VALHALLA

THE

MYTHS OF NORSELAND

𝔄 𝔖𝔞𝔤𝔞, 𝔦𝔫 𝔗𝔴𝔢𝔩𝔳𝔢 𝔓𝔞𝔯𝔱𝔰

BY

JULIA CLINTON JONES

Faded the Twilight of the gods
Thro' the wild lands of the North ;
From phœnix-fire a God far higher,
Our Christ-Child cometh forth

———⁂———

Fredonia Books
Amsterdam, The Netherlands

Valhalla:
The Myths of Norseland

by
Julia Clinton Jones

ISBN: 1-58963-889-1

Reprinted from the 1878 edition

Fredonia Books
Amsterdam, The Netherlands
http://www.fredoniabooks.com

TO THE READER.

To avoid a multiplicity of foot notes, an appendix has been prepared, which will be found at end of book, to which the reader is referred for all allusions and proper names.

CONTENTS.

PREFACE.

WHAT a curious fact it is, that among us, English speaking people, scholarly investigation has clung rather to the classic lore and mythology of Greece and Rome, than to the less classic, but far purer and truer religion of the North.

It is much to be deplored that so slight a knowledge of Scandinavian Mythology prevails, popularly, with those who boast descent from Hengist and Horsa, and whose pride it is that in their veins flows the blood that long ago thrilled through the bold hearts of the Vikings, descendants of the old Norse-Gods.

While still Thor and Odin, Tyr and Freya give names to our week-days;—while still many finger-posts of language and legend, custom and super-stition, point us back to the times of Skald and Saga, when our ancestors sang their runic rhymes in groves of oak around the sacrificial stone, and worshiped Nature's forces;—here, among us, sprung chiefly of Teutonic races, but little is known of their lore and religion.

That this mythology *was* the religion of our fore-fathers, should be an incentive to our careful study of it, casting aside the additional fact of its own interest, grandeur, and beauty.

The very foundations of the Gothic faith lay in principles of temperance, freedom, and chastity; bravery and justice were its key-stones; through valiant deeds alone could Valhalla, their Heaven, be won by its votaries. What wonder then, im-bued with such doctrines, the part these Norsemen played in early European history,—the mighty turn they gave to the broad current of civilization.

Fired by threat of subjugation, roused by the advancing strides of conquering Cæsar, they rushed like an avalanche from their snow-capped fastnesses, to fall upon Rome, and wrest away her servile dependencies,—to teach unto men the grand doctrines of freedom and moral obligations;—then, as Goth and Teuton, Frank and Saxon, to form new states, with liberty as the basis of their laws, and toleration and justice their crowning glory.

They found Rome weakened by conquest, and enervated by luxury; one by one they forced her conquests from her, plunging Europe into a state of semi-barbarism, only to raise her up at last, through their stronger northern natures, and purer institutions to a higher degree of enlightenment; infusing through her weakened frame, their own bold blood, thus giving her fresh strength and vitality.

But, after all, when Goth and Teuton, Frank and Saxon, had trampled upon principalities in their resistless course,—when they had established those dynasties whose successors to-day hold the reins of power,—it needed the defiant daring, the indomitable spirit of the Norsemen to counteract the more phlegmatic natures of their southern kinsmen.

Instigated as they were by the teachings of their Æsir-faith,—animated by the example of their hero-gods,—inspired by mythical prophecy,—what wonder that we find them carrying out these teachings and prophecies, undaunted by danger or the fear of death.

The broad Atlantic proved no bar to their progress, and the first European who trod American soil was a Norseman.

Alps nor Pyrenees raised a barrier to their headlong course. Savage as they were in those early days, rude and ferocious, although brave and generous, they were a terror to the more polished inhabitants of the luxurious provinces of the South.

Italy quailed before these long-beards; Greece trembled as they advanced, chanting the runes of the North.

Up to the very gates of Jerusalem they pressed; nor were they unknown on the coasts of Africa. Their footsteps echoed through the streets of Constantinople; while the white sails of their ships wafted them over the blue waves of the Mediterranean, anchoring off the conquered coasts of Apulia and Sicily.

Until, at last, their very name became a threat, and from church and town went up the prayer, embodied in one of the Litanies of the day, "From the fury of the Northmen, good Lord, deliver us!"

Planting wherever they trod, the germs of a glorious freedom, they were the revolutionists of that age, and all succeeding ages owe them a lasting debt of gratitude for the noble harvest that has sprung up from the seeds of liberty and truth by them sown.

To their scorn of luxurious feebleness,—to their unswerving love of temperance and morality, do we to-day owe that which has led us on from height to height,—the principles which have placed England in the foremost rank of the nations, and which are blazoned forth on the glorious flag of her daughter, our own United States.

Not from conquered Britain, or enslaving Rome, then, came the leaders who roused England to deeds of greatness and glory,—but from the frozen fens and rugged shores of the far-off North, the sons of Thor and Odin rushed to sustain her faltering van.

The climate and face of a country unquestionably influence the physical peculiarities of its people, likewise that people's moral characteristics; so

Mythology, being a deification of natural phenom-
ena, materially partakes of the nature of the climate
and face of the country where it is nurtured and
matured,—itself only a reflex of the mind of the
people among whom it originates.

Thus, the Southerner, in whose land nature revels
in beauty, and whose clime woos to ease and luxury,
became effeminate and sensuous; with him, then,
religion was pleasure and self-indulgence.

While, lost in the contemplation of the ice-bound
peaks of his native land,—Creation's earliest land-
marks,—the Norseman's hardy spirit was lifted up
from earth to the thought of a higher existence;
thus did his nature become nobler and more aspiring
through contact with his grander, bolder surround-
ings, and so gave birth to a purer Mythology.   Held
fast in the arms of the great Mother, he counted
each pulse-beat of her mighty heart, and imbibed
renewed life and vigor from this close communion.

Religion, with him, became a craving after a fuller
life, one to which this world is but the threshold.
The heaven of the Greek was on earth; *his* mind
could soar no higher than Olympus; *Valhalla* rested
among the clouds, and the death-river Thund,
flowed before its gates.

In that dim Elder-Day, the untaught mind of the Norseman, not guided by the light of Science as ours now is, and hence unable to trace the intricate workings of the scheme of Nature, ascribed each part of the system, to the particular agency of some peculiar deity, and, as the forces were friendly or unfriendly to him, he either worshiped them as gods, or dreaded them as Jötuns. To him, the roaring of the storm was the coming of angry Thor, the thunder of whose chariot wheels shakes the universe, while his eyes flash fierce lightnings.

Fire, to him, was the demon Loki; whose evil nature breaks forth in the volcano;—who, in a wider sense, was Lucifer himself.

While again, in Frost and Ice, he recognized giants, monstrous, and most terrible.

In earth, he found Friga, the loving Mother, wedded to Odin, the Al-father, Lord of heavenly Asgard. The various changes of the seasons, were set forth in mythic forms, and beautifully were the different duties and personalities of the gods displayed. The Norseman looked forward to his Ragnarock with unquestioning faith, and hoped for a happy resurrection. He believed that through

destruction alone could come regeneration,—
through death, a higher life. Bright-winged
Valkyriar bore him to Valhalla after a hero-death,
or the black Dragon, Nidhögg, dragged him down to
Naströnd, if base or cowardly. So did he recognize
Heaven and Hell. In so many respects did the
Norse religion coincide with the Bible dispensation,
that its followers long resisted the introduction of
Christianity; it was only after the announcement
that the old gods were dead that Christ was accepted
with His mild and holy teachings. It is now, with
great pleasure, that I place before the reader these
few following fables from distant frozen lands, feeling
assured that he will delight, even as I have done,
in the poetry of their imagery, and in the grand
truths that shine forth through their mythic lore.
Concerning the signification which I have attached
to these myths, I must state that other explanations
are likewise given, that often they are rendered as
natural and physical, rather than as spiritual allusions. Still, I love to think that the bold Vikings,
those strong-souled heroes of Eld, went deeper into
the grand scheme of Creation, and recognized the
power of God working in the heart of Nature, in a

fuller sense than in the mere Jötun force displayed in the earthquake shock, or tempest blast. In the analogies drawn below, I wish to show the very close similitude between what we are taught by the Church to regard as her peculiar doctrines, and the Mythology of the North, whose origin is involved in the obscurity of past ages.

Let us accept these myths as glimmerings of that light which shines in perfect day for us.

From the beginning was God, and in various forms, all men have acknowledged Him.

Throughout these myths, the old Skalds and Sagas have striven to evolve the truth dimly shining before them. Throughout runs a double thread—as in the relation of Odin and Friga, Divinity acting upon earthly powers,—in the story of Baldur, the innocent Sun-God, and in the personifications of Loki's children,—a double thread, spiritual and physical.

The Norsemen looked from Nature up to Nature's God, and seeing the various forms and changes of the great Mother, applied them to divinity, and thence to that lesser type of a sublimer being,—man, spiritually, and physically.

And through all we may trace the creating and protecting Trinity of the Christian system;—the great frame-work of the religion of Christ with its final Judgment and Resurrection.

Whether the same with the Greek, and borrowed from it, or whether drawn from a pure Aryan foun·tain-head under Indian skies, still the seeds of truth are there.

———

In the beginning was Muspel, Niflheim, and Ginunga,—Fire, Darkness, and Chaos.

Muspel and Niflheim, meeting in Ginunga, pro·duced the first formless Jötun matter, Ymir,—the world-mass. From Chaos then sprang gods, those Powers of Good,—creative and protective,—and, at the same time came Jötuns,—Beings of Ill, dis·turbing and deadly.

In the beginning commenced the strife between Good and Ill.

The Æsir-Trinity,—Odin, Vili, and Vè,—de·stroyed the Frost-Giants, (destructive natural ele·ments); then, from Ymir created Earth, and formed Man, each in his own image. So Divinity went forth in a three-fold form, and, the great work of

Creation being complete, in Odin (the Soul of the Universe) were the Three blended. In Valhalla, the Æsir-Heaven, assembled the gods,—all personifications of divine or earthly powers.

Thence they watched over Midgard (Earth).

Their various adventures are but mythical representations of the strife between Light and Darkness, Spirit and Matter, Virtue and Vice;—Nature disturbed by natural causes of ill, and man's soul torn by lusts and evil passions.

Among the Æsir crept in the bad Loki, one with Odin at the first, under the form of Vili, spiritual fire; but, like Lucifer fallen from above, he descended on earth, and became an evil flame, cruel and devastating.

While on earth, he was the parent of the Serpent, the Wolf, and Hela,—Sin, Pain, and Death,—whom the Gods strove to bind in the Abyss, but could only cast down for a time. They were born in the dragon's bed, and nourished on the dew of dwarfs,—personifications, each, of gold.

So it was that the lust of riches was the nurse and promoter of ills and troubles in the world.

Until Loki fell, Earth was as Eden.

Loki and his brood were also the chief causes of physical disturbances, and their demon natures burst forth in the earthquake and volcano, the tempest and conflagration.

Baldur, the Sun-God, was Innocence,—the Light of the world, quenched by Hœder (blind, physical strength,—Ignorance), lured on by the tempter Loki (sin). Baldur being slain, his loving wife Nanna (the desire for all good things) was buried with him.

Then was born Vali (Repentance), who was the swift avenger of his brother.

Still, although Mother Earth (Friga) with all Creation, except sinful Loki, mourned for Baldur, Hela held him fast. Innocence, once dead, could return no more until the Regeneration.

Baldur is often the personification of the summer sun slain by the long dark winter of the North.

Loki, imprisoned in the Abyss, left behind him numerous progeny,—ills and woes that should torment the world, and continue the strife that would end only in the final destruction.

Odin and Hela divided man between them.

The spirit went forth from the Æsir-Trinity,—the body (the tree) sprang from the Jötun-World,—

so, from the beginning, Odin and Hela contended for dominion over humanity. Valkyriar (bright angels) led hero souls to Odin, to await the final battle when they should fight with him against the hosts of Hela,—those worthless and sin-stricken ones, brought to her by the dread Death-Dragon.

For this World-Life struggle ended in one great conflict, in which opposing powers mutually destroyed each other, and involved the world itself in the general ruin.

Igdrasil, the Life-Tree, withered in the flames,— for Time shall end at the Judgment-Day.

As Loki was received in Asgard, so was Lucifer cherished in Heaven.

As Loki descended on earth, and there brought forth the Serpent, the Wolf, and Hela, to be the tormentors of Midgard, so Lucifer fell from his high estate, and Sin, Pain, and Death, scourges of earth, are his offspring.

Can we not, in Baldur, see an image, faint perhaps, of that pure One on whom, too, Innocence brooded like a dove,—the Christ slain by that Iscariot who purposed not His death, but blindly sold Him for the reward of betrayal? While who is Loki, but the temper Satan, who ever stands behind with evil counsel?

Likewise, as Gabriel with flaming sword stands at the Gate of Heaven, so stood Heimdal at Asgard's portal; and as he, in dreadful Ragnarock, sounded the summons on great Gjallar-horn,—so shall Gabriel with his trump, call the quick and the dead to judgment.

As Ragnarock came to the Norseman with its storms, and conflagrations, and strife,—when the chainēd Loki was loosed,—when Ægir and Ran led out their bands of the Drowned to join with Hela's hosts against Odin and his hero-array;—when Surtur cast forth his fire, and in the great World-Blaze all ended, and Igdrasil's self was consumed;—even so to *us* comes our Day of Doom, when "Satan shall be loosed out of his prison; when the sea shall give up her dead, and death and hell deliver up the dead that are in them; when there shall be war in Heaven, and Michael and his angels shall fight against the Dragon, whose angels shall fight with him; when the earth shall be consumed, and the heavens depart as a scroll when it is rolled together; and when time shall be no more."

And last, these old myth s held orth the promise of a glorious regeneration,—new heavens, and a new earth, with a purer race of Æsir, and a golden-roofed Gimli.

To us, likewise shall come a resurrection, when "former things are passed away,"—when a new earth, and a new heaven shall be prepared for us also,—a new Jerusalem whose streets are pure gold.

Then shall come to all,—Norseman and Christian alike, and to those who dwell in the uttermost parts of the earth,—the High and Mighty One, whose name no man dare utter, who existed from the beginning,—the creative spark of life from Muspel,—and He who said, "Let there be light;" the God of Gods, and Judge of all men, who shall call the good to His glorious golden Throne in highest Heaven, and cast the wicked below to the gloomy habitation of Hell, where the Dragon shall prey on them forever and ever, and where they shall dwell in tor. ment. As by the flames of Surtur's sword did purification come to the Æsir-Creation; — so, through fire alone shall Earth be purified, and Death be overcome.

As fair Iduna alone had never touched Loki's

foul brood, so she alone passed unscathed through Surtur's flames. And so shall Immortality rise above Death, and stand forevermore in Heaven's eternal Gate.

VALHALLA.

PART FIRST.

CREATION.

IN the dim morning-dawn of Time,
   E'er yet was made the green Earth fair,
   With Muspel bright, and dark Niflheim,
   Ginunga, still as windless air,—
These three,—two Worlds of Fire and Night
With the Abyss,—ruled in their might.

Great Surtur, with his burning sword,
Southward, at Muspel's gate kept ward,
   And flashes of celestial flame.

Life-giving, from the Fire-World came;
While in the North, in Niflheim dread,
Dwelt Nidhögg, Dragon of the Dead;
Death-dealing frosts and vapors rise
From that black Mist-World, full of sighs.
Between the two, Ginunga lay,
A yawning chasm void of day.
The salt rime-drops from Niflheim's streams
Quickened by Muspel's living beams,
Met in Ginunga's gloomy space,
And Ymir bore, of Jötun race,
Who of himself Hrimthursar had,—
Frost-Giants they, and Jötuns' bad.

The Cow, Audhumla, having nursed
The Jötun Ymir, licked the rime;
Just wrath to wreak on the accursed,
Then forth sprang Buri, the Divine.
From Bör, his son, came Æsir three,
Odin, and Vili, and great Vè,
Who, slaying Ymir in fierce war,
Drowned in his blood the Hrimthursar.

Now was conceived the god-like plan;—
The Spirit, Light, and mighty Fire,

Those Æsir three, their task began,—
Creation's wondrous work entire.
From Asgard's Hill, their heavenly home,
The sons of Bör triumphant come!
Into Ginunga, Ymir hurled;
Out of his parts they formed the World;
His body, Earth; his blood, the Sea;
Mountains, his bones; each hair, a tree;
They of his skull created sky,
Above the Earth fair archēd high,
Adorned with sparks from Muspel bright,—
The Sun, and Moon, and stars of light;
While, for defence 'gainst Jötun raid,
A breast-work of his eye-brows made,
And called it Midgard, and acrost
From Asgard, threw the bridge Bifröst,—
The Rainbow-bridge of colors three,—
That joined with Heaven, Earth might be.
Around the Earth they caused to swell
Deep seas upon whose utmost strand,
Jötuns escaped they gave to dwell
In black and fearful nether land.

Of Jötun race sprang black-browed Night
Who unto bright-eyed Day gave birth;
Him Æsir placed in car of light
Darkness to chase away from Earth;
Hence Night and Day alternate course
The heav'ns in circle-wise, perforce.
Night rides before on dark Hrimfax,
Who hoar-frost from his bridle shakes;
While, from Skinfaxi's mane so fair,
Day scatters light o'er earth and air.
Lest Jötun wolves should them devour,
To swiftest flight they bend each power.

The Sun, beneath the sultry noon,
Held, high in Heaven, her horse's rein;
And, with her pale companion, Moon,
Waited until the gods should deign
To mark their path, their powers to tell,
And place the stars from bright Muspel.

Born in the flesh of Ymir old,
Four dwarfs the mighty Æsir set
Four corners of the sky to hold;

While, where the outmost boundaries met,
The giant Hræ, in eagle guise
Sat in the north,—when he shall rise,
Each mighty wing-stroke will give birth
To storms that desolate the Earth.

Within, below, o'ershadowing all,
The Life-Tree, Igdrasil, upreared
Its sacred boughs o'er Asgard's Hall,
Alike by gods and Jötuns feared.
Its Nornir sat by Odin's gate,
Spinning the thread of Time and Fate;
While deeper down was Mimir's Well
On which was laid rare Wisdom's spell;
Its deepest root did Nidhögg gnaw,
Dragon of Death! forever more.
Hovered aloft the Eagle, Life,
While deep below lurked Death and Strife.

From high Valhalla's hall of might,
The Æsir looked the whole Earth o'er,
Did in their handiwork delight;
And then, upon the lone sea-shore
Seeing two trees, the Ash and Elm,

They chose them rulers of this realm,
Lest all the fair Creation vast
Be wasted, lonely, to the last.
Odin on them the Spirit poured,
And sense was their's by Vili's word;
With flesh, and speech, and sight were they
Endowed by power of mighty Vè.
*He Ask, she Embla, they by name,
First Man and Woman now became.
On Midgard did the glorious Three
Place human life and destiny.

And now the gods' great work was o'er.
Creation, beautiful, complete,
The vaulted sky, the sea-girt shore
Lay, stretched along at Odin's feet.
But even in this early morn,
Faintly foreshadowed, was the dawn
Of that fierce struggle, deadly shock,
Which yet should end in Ragnarock ;
When Good and Evil, Death and Life,
Beginning now, end then their strife.

* The Elder Edda ascribes the creation of man not to the sons of Bör,
but to another trinity of gods,—Odin, Hœnir, and Lödur, probably th
same as Odin, Baldur, and Loki.

PART SECOND.

VALHALLA.

ALL is ended! all is done,—
  Every thing beneath the sun;
While above,—the stars, the sky,—
  Even Valhal, home on high
Of the gods', in Asgard's land,—
  Full-perfected now doth stand.

  Assemble, ye gods!
  In Valhalla's high hall
  Odin awaits ye,
  Seats stand for ye all.

Valhalla's high hall, 'gainst wild tempest proof
Spears are its pillars, and shields are its roof!
    Battle-axes carve the feast,
    Coats of mail for ev'ry guest
    Drape the walls, support the board;
Valhalla, home of Odin, God,
On Asgard's height, is the delight
Of Æsir, working deeds of might.

The Eagle of great Igdrasil
High hovers o'er the sacred Hill,
        Bird of Life!
        While waves of strife
Round the gates of Asgard pour,—
Loud hear Thund, the Death-Stream, roar!
    'Thro' the dreadful tumult made,
    Fallen heroes hither wade,
    Brought to Odin by Valkyr,
    Battle-maidens held most dear.
        O'er sea and thro' air,
        'Mid lightnings' fierce glare,
            Bright shields bearing,
            Each maid wearing

Gleaming armor, side by side,
Down thro' lurid sky they ride.
When to Asgard back they come,
Tyr and Vidar welcome home;
 Valhal's wide hall
 Has room for all!
Odin loves not empty seat;
Fairest maids the victors greet,
Fill full high with mead the bowl,—
Deeply drinks each warrior soul.

High in Valhal sits God Odin;
 By his side, in place of pride,
Decked with falcon plumes is Friga, —
 Queen of gods, and Odin's bride ;
  Æsir's Mother,
  Fjörgyn's daughter !
Future is to her revealed
Useless, for her lips are sealed.

  And now, at last
  Thro' Heav'n the blast
Rings clear from Heimdal's mighty horn
O'er earth and air its sound is borne.

Loud summons the Æsir,—
Gods of the earth and air,—
To Valhalla's glorious feast;
Fading faint the sound has ceased.

First, Thor with the bent brow,
In red beard muttering low,
Darting fierce lightnings from eye-balls that glow,
Comes, while each chariot-wheel
Echoes in thunder-peal,
As his dread hammer-shock
Makes Earth and Heaven rock,
Clouds rifting above, while Earth quakes below.

Fairest of all gods, beautiful Baldur!
Bright-browed and pure One, best loved of Æsir
Light from his shining face
Streams over Asgard's race;
Rising from realms of night,
Bears he in car of light,
Bears he from realms afar,
Brilliantly beaming, joy to Valhalla!

Why trembles Friga on her throne
When comes blind Hœdur, Odin's son?
Lo! strong and silent drawing near,
The Mother shrinks from him in fear,
  For of veiled Futurity
  Pierces she the mystery;
  Baldur's fate to her revealed
  Useless, since her lips are sealed.

  Now Loki comes, cause of ill!
  Men and Æsir curse him still.
   Long shall the gods deplore,
   Even till Time be o'er,
  His base fraud on Asgard's Hill.
While, deep in Jötunheim, most fell,
Are Fenrir, Serpent, and dread Hel, —
Pain, Sin and Death, his children three,—
Brought up and cherished; thro' them he
Tormentor of the world shall be.

  Lovely Gerda, Goddess rare!
  Snow white arms and bosom fair
  Gleaming soft o'er sea and air!

With her brilliant beaming blush,
Glowing lights thro' cloud-waves rush
While Auroras from her hair
Quiver 'round the ether dome;
Shooting o'er the Northern skies
Radiant arrows from her eyes,
As to Odin's joyous home,
She, the Bride of Frey, doth come.

Great Frey himself hastens hither,
Lord of warm, life-giving weather!
Soft-dropping rains
O'er smiling plains,
And dew-drops shed
On Nature's bed,
Fall from his chariot, fleet and bright,
As speeds he on to halls of light.

Bright Iduna, Maid immortal!
Standing at Valhalla's portal,
In her casket has rich store
Of rare apples, gilded o'er;
Those rare apples, not of Earth,
Ageing Æsir give fresh birth.

When e'er the fearful Day be past,—
That Day, of Odin's pow'r the last,—
   She, unharmed shall stand the shock,
   Rising over Ragnarock,
Defying Surtur, God of Fire,
Conqu'ring Serpent, Hel and Fenrir;
   Then, to Gimli's golden dome,
   Lead the purer Æsir home.

     Amid the summons loud,
     Rising o'er Earth and cloud,
Swelling, then lying faint on ambient air,
   In rich melodious strain
   The rune-notes' sweet refrain
Falls ling'ring, from the golden harp-strings rare!
     Ecstatic notes!
     Each, liquid floats
   In welcome as the Æsir come;
     Circling round Odin's home,
     Up to Valhalla's dome,
   Triumphant, exultant, they rise;
     E'er they reel and rebound
     In full billows of sound.

Thrilling greetings thro' trembling skies, —
  Rare greetings o'er rain-bow arch,
  As hither the Æsir march,
    Still Bragi doth sing;
    Higher and louder,
    Clearer and prouder,
    Entrancing chords ring!
   Seated at Odin's feet,
   Pouring forth floods of sweet
    Silvery sound,
   Bragi, on Idun's breast,
   Singing shall ever rest;
  Soft strains from skilled finger-tips,
  High themes from wise rune-graved lips
    Echo around!
Delighting with his minstrelsy
The gods amid their revelry,
  Until Surtur's fiery brand
  Ruin flings o'er sea and land;
Then, passed the Twilight of the gods,
E'er shall he dwell in pure abodes,
And, beyond all reach of sadness,
He shall pour forth notes of gladness.

In that radiant hall of state
Decorated seats are set,
Still with gore the swords are wet.
　　No craven there
　　To sit may dare !
In the brightness of the gods,
In those blessēd, grand abodes,
Heroes feast, on couches lying,
Brave in life, most blest in dying.

Close beside him, in the Feast-hall,
　Stand the beauteous Maids of War,
Who from the stricken field shall call
　Bands of strong Einheriar.
Grave they wait, with bright shields gleaming
　Thoughtful, brazen spears in hand,
Of those chosen Norse-sons dreaming,
　Soon to feast with Odin's band.

Whispered Odin, "Soon the gray Wolf
　In Valhalla shows his face ;
Who can tell how soon in Vingolf
　He shall ravage Asgard's race ?

More triumphant then the rune,
Sweeter far will be the tune
Than now in Valhal
At high festival,
When with Iduna, then shall he
The Æsir greet full joyously,
As the fierce strife on Vigrid's plain
Rolls away,
And Odin's race shall meet again
In brighter day.

Feasting and pleasure,
Joy without measure
In Valhalla hold full sway;
While, throughout the happy day,
To and fro goes Hermodur,—
O'er the Earth, and thro' the air
Swift and sure, as messenger,
Odin's mandates oft doth bear.

For even in the flowing bowl
Shall ne'er forget the god-like soul;
Æsir great
All await
Until Heimdal sounds his call.

Valhalla's feast
Enchains no guest!
When there is need,
No sparkling mead,
Nor maiden's kiss,
Nor Asgard's bliss
Keeps them in Valhalla's hall.

To their power belongs
To quell evil, right wrongs!
Earth lifts to them her pleading hands,
For them, Air stills his tempest bands,
While Dwarf with Jötun trembling stands
All bow before their high commands,
By purity made strong.

So the gods in glorious state,
Dwell within Valhalla's gate.
Cursed be the woeful hour
When shall creep in Jötun power,
When Good and Ill, in deadly shock
Shall battle in dread Ragnarock.

PART THIRD.

EINHERIAR'S SONG.

FEASTING sit the mighty Æsir
    In Valhalla's golden splendor :
There, on snow-white arm reclining,
Garlands gay is Freya twining ;
    " Mercy," singeth Baldur bright,
    " Is the ornament of might.
As wreaths bedeck the victor's shield,
So Mercy crowns him on the field."

Thronēd high is Odin great ;
Well he loves the Hero-feast :
Wounds adorn each warrior guest.

Still seats are empty.   Go ye forth
    Thro' the kingdoms of the North ;
Bold warriors who have bravely fought,
    Mighty deeds have nobly wrought,
Choose ye from the misty Norse-land,
    Allies, at our Throne to stand ;
So, when fierce Fenrir comes in might,
    They may aid us in the fight.
Heroic deed claims god-like meed,
Of valiant hearts have Æsir need.
            Daughters of War !
            Scent ye afar
        Where red battle doth rage,
        The steam of the carnage.
            Who on the death-plain
            Hath striven to gain
Peace for his country, and fame for his gods,
Bring here on your shields to blessed abodes,
            E'er in victorious festival
            To sup with us in high Valhal."

            Swift thro' the startled air,
            Like lightning flashing,

Thro' war-clouds dashing,
Speed the Valkyriar !
Brazen armor gleaming bright,
Glittering far with Glory's light,
*Skuld, their leader, upward lifting
Pointing finger, where, thro' rifting
Crimson clouds, the path is lying
To the gods in glorious dying.

Louder the battle roars !
As rain the life-blood pours !
Shivers the barbed lance !
Sharp swords like meteors glance!
Each fiery heart
Pierced by Death's dart
Exults with sluggish life to part !
Fiercer yet see warriors battling,
Twanging bows and quivers rattling ;
Thro' the field, mad chargers rushing,
Ruthless hoofs the fallen crushing ;
O'er red earth, with strong spears crashing
Gold haired sons of valiant sires

*Skuld—Norna of the Future

Like their northern blasts are dashing;
In each breast, Berserker fires

   Spring hot to life
    At sound of strife,
 Smell of blood their sinews bracing,
 Film of death from glazed eyes chasing;
  Leaping mad thro' hostile bands,
  Seizing victory with fierce hands,
  Clutching in wild grasp, the spear
  Which shall wide their heart-strings tear;
 Triumphant, feel the welcome wound
 That, sure, the seat of life has found;
 Falling on the field of slaughter
 Wildly screaming joyful laughter,
 Exultant, that in Saga's song,
 Undying, should their deeds belong;
 Impatient, hail the maids who bear
 Their souls aloft on blood-shields rare.

Downward thro' gore and carnage swooping,
Valkyriar, o'er the death-field stooping,—
   The field of fame.—

In Odin's name,
Choose from the slain
On whom the hero-mark is plain.
On their brows press icy kisses,
Hold them close in cold embraces,
Snatch them from the arms of Death,
Woo back life with Glory's breath.
Back streams their golden hair
As thro' the trembling air,
Up to the Æsir,
The bold Valkyriar
On gory shields their spirits bear.
Heimdal waits at Asgard's portal,
Leads to Idun, Maid Immortal.
Gaping wounds are bound by Eyra
Ee'r they feast with blue-eyed Freya.
Then, loud the song of triumph rings,—
'Tis Bragi, lo! the rune who sings!

————

BRAGI'S SONG.

"Skoal to the Heroes, from battle returning!
Loud sung for aye be each death-dealing blow

With scorning, to Hel, the craven ones spurning,
  Shield-bearing Valkyrs exultantly go.
Agape are the wounds, proud crimson marks glowing,
  Gashes of glory on Heroes who die ;
Precious to Odin, the purple tide flowing,
  Each red drop, a wine-draught, runes ev'ry sigh.
Fires of Conquest, the dun skies are lighting,
  Vidar is chaunting victorious strain ;
Hail to our Feast-Hall ! great Heimdal, inviting,
  On Gjallar-horn sounds triumphant refrain.
Mercy and Might round each bold heart are twining,
  Adorning each soul like shield-graven blooms ;
Gondula and Skuld, with Rota, combining,
  Bear them to Vingolf, thro' Death's welcome
    glooms.
Odin awaits them, in splendor proud sitting,
  There gather the gods in high festival ;
Vidar and Thor shall receive as befitting
  Einheriar led to golden Valhal.
Radiant couches for them are preparing,
  Banquets that strengthen the warrior-soul ;
Maidens alluring full beakers are bearing,—
  Love mingling with wine in o'erflowing bowl.
Softly recline they on warm bosoms, thrilling

Every quick pulse of the swift throbbing heart ;
Fulla for Friga their mead-cups high filling,—
  Joy is imperfect where Love hath no part.
Safely surrounded by Passion's sweet longing,
  Feast they and rest they till dawning of light ;
Pleasure and banquet to Valor belonging,
  Feasting shall strengthen strong sinews of Might
Then when the car of fair Day is uprising
  From dense murky depths of cloud-land below,
On Idavöld's plain, in warfare surprising,
  Till eve shall they strive, in prowess shall grow.
So, when the gray wolf to Asgard be coming,
  And Jötun hosts rage in wild tempest shock,
For Odin they'll fight, in Day of dark dooming,
  And battle for him, in dread Ragnarock."

        So Bragi ends ; thro' list'ning air
        Rise, swell, and die, the rune-notes rare.
        Around the Hall, on seats of gold
        Recline at ease Einheriar bold.
        Bright maids, caressing, pour the mead,
        While Saga chaunts each warlike deed ;
        On Bragi's breast, Iduna leans,

Fair Gerda's blush thro' Valhal gleams,
And Friga welcomes to her side
The Hero-band, great Odin's pride.
In joy and feasting, passes night;
Their souls, with dawn rejoice in fight;
They, blest, shall dwell in fair abodes
Till comes the Twilight of the gods;
'Gainst Hela, and her hosts of Dead,
They then shall strive in battle dread.

PART FOURTH.

LOKI, THE MISCHIEF MAKER.

'NEATH Valhalla's glorious dome,
In the Æsir's heavenly home,
Hither, hence, they ceaseless roam,
Rest to find, their labors done ;
Rest and pleasure
Without measure !
Finished task is pleasure won.
In fair Duty's perfect round,
Godlike souls are ever found.

From beaming day till cloudless night
The gods compete in works of might ;

Great Friga's bounteous smiles delight
And warm the Earth; Frey, from his height,
  Sunshine and rain
  O'er hill and plain,
  Sends to the Earth,
  That plenteous birth
From Nature's womb may deck his fane.
Lovely Gerda's brilliant blushes,
Lights auroral, quiv'ring flushes,
From Frey's proud throne, thro' evening air,
Tremble in ether wavelets rare.
The grateful Earth looks up with love
To bright Valhalla's dome above;
While, in dark Jötunheim most drear,
Giants and dwarfs shrink down in fear.

  Love is the rule of all
  In Valhalla's high hall!
Love is the Lord! Love never fails!
  Meekness and strength,
  Mingled at length,
By Love poised in Odin's just scales.

So Love ruled all
    Till Loki's fall,—
Loki, thro' whom Death, Sin and Woe
Should ravage Heaven, and Earth below.
One with Odin at the first
When the grand Creation burst
From the Æsir's glorious plan ;
One with him when Time began ;
One with him in godlike thought ;
One with him in good deeds wrought ;
    At every feast
    His honored guest ;
    His foster-brother,
    Of Jötun mother ;
Fair of face, seductive grace,
Fair, as tho' of Æsir race,—
Fell he from his high estate.
Sinking in the depths of Earth,
There had Loki second birth,—
Born of Laufey, frail and base ;
    His father, Wind,
    Fickle, unkind ;
Dwelt he within Utgard's gate.
Thro' Jötun change, his holy fire

Burnt fiercer into wrong desire,
Mingling with evil ones, became
An earthly, devastating flame.

   Deep below, on dragon's bed,
   Brought he forth his children dread,
   Frightful, fearful, fiendish brood !
   Loving evil, hating good ;
Wily Serpent, raging Fenrir,
Dark Hel most awful, scourges drear,
     Shapes so terrible,
     Forms too horrible
For aught but wretched Guilt to see,
Yet ever in the world to be ;
While in fierce Loki's deepest soul
Held he most dear these offspring foul.

Now back to Asgard having come,
The gods receive the traitor home.
Little the mighty Æsir dream
Their brother be not all he seem,
     But prone to hate
     Their better state ;
Ah ! bitter have the high gods cursed
The evil stock which Loki nursed !

Goes he where the Æsir go,
Working still as secret foe
To undo their mighty deeds;
Leaves them at their greatest needs
Now soon in Asgard peace is dead!
From Valhalla rest has fled.
    Creeping in
    Shapes of sin,
Lust of gold and greed of gain,
Dim the light on Ida's plain.
Darkly, densely gather there
Forms that seem of thinnest air,
But as yet that show all fair;—
Hateful forms, by Loki brought,
Which shall render Asgard naught!

    Ever by stealth
    Works he himself,
Foul and fiendish like his race;
    All woes that fall
    On Odin's hall
Can be traced to Loki base.
From out Valhalla's portal
'Twas he who pure Iduna lured,—

Whose casket fair
Held apples rare
That render gods immortal,—
And in Thiassi's tower immured.

By his mocking, scornful mien,
Soon, in Valhal it was seen
'Twas the traitor Loki's art
Which had led Idun apart
To gloomy tower,
And Jötun power.
In eagle guise he wrought the wrong ;
In like disguise the wrathful throng
Of Æsir force him bring the maid
Safe under Asgard's mighty shade,
Guarded by god-like power most strong.

Once did the traitor rank conspire
'Gainst Asgard's mighty host entire ;
At one fell blow
To wreak dread woe.
Tho' trusted by the Æsir still,
'Twas Loki planned the hateful ill.
To Asgard came an architect,

And castle offered to erect,—
    A castle high
    Which should defy
Deep Jötun guile and giant raid ;
And this most wily compact made,—
Fair Freya, with the Moon and Sun
As price the fortress being done.
Darkened, indeed, and gloomy all
Earth, Asgard, and Valhalla's hall,
Should aught the Moon or Sun befall ;
Barren the earth, breathless the air,
If they should lose loved Freya's care !

    Deceitful wile,
    Seducing guile
So well had veiled the deep-laid scheme
The gods could not detect, nor dream
Which one of all Valhalla's throng
Had been the author of the wrong,
Till, like a flash, the memory came,—
'Twas *Loki* did the payment name !

Horror and fear the gods beset ;
Finished almost the castle stood !

In three days more
The work be o'er ;
Then must they make their contract good,
And pay the awful debt.

Horror and fear
At danger near
Sudden to fiercest anger turned ;
Each god-like soul now eager burned
To force him break the contract dread,
Or vengeance wreak on Loki's head.
Guile and fear are kindred ever,
Brothers they, who may not sever !
To appease the Æsir ire
Loki bent to their desire,
That crafty builder's strongest stay,
The magic steed, to wile away.
Subtile and full of strange device,
As a young mare did he entice
The horse afar to unknown shore ;
Thus could the plotter harm no more.
Thro' all the night,
Till morning's light,

Swift after Svadelfari fleet
The Builder sped with anxious feet.

But useless all !   By Loki foiled,
His anger on the gods recoiled,
As further work himself could naught
Without the magic aid he brought.
Now, casting all disguise aside,
Amidst the gods in angry pride,—
While crumbling sank the half-built tower
In giant form and Jötun power
He stood !   Wild terror seized on all,
Lest ruin should on Asgard fall.

Dread hour for Valhal ! help was none
When Asgard's stoutest stay was gone !
The vengeful Jötun, tow'ring high,
With scoffing taunt and furious cry,
Shook gate and roof—e'en upper sky,—
    Grasped at the Sun,
    While pallid Moon
    Coursed swiftly by !
Then on the trembling Æsir turned,
    And forward dashed :

In thunders crashed
Portal and wall, defences they
Too feeble all in such affray,—
Like reeds from out his path he spurned.

But, joy! great Thor, returning slow
  From road and toil
  And frequent broil,
  In wearied march
  Up rainbow arch,
Heard the foul insults of the foe.
Frantic at the outrage wrought,
Maddened by the ruin sought,
As storm-wind sudden, on he swept,
Like thunder-bolt on Jötun leapt!
As on the giant foe he sprang,
'Gainst rib and thigh great Mjölnir rang,
  With mighty stroke
  His skull he broke,—
Then hurled him down to Hel below.

So Thor restored Valhalla's peace.
But ills in Asgard did not cease;
Uneven balanced Odin's scales.

Kindness on evil nature fails,
          Meekness naught avails !
          Odin's self, distraught
          By the trouble wrought,
Early and late e'er sought from Fate
Wisdom to rule in god-like state.

PART FIFTH.

MIMIR'S WELL.

IN the dread Frost-Giants' dwelling,
    In the realm of Jötunheim,
By the sacred Life Tree swelling,
    Filled with mysteries of Time,
The Fountain sprang of Mimir wise,—
Mimir, knowing good and ill,—
While from those silver waves would rise
Mists that watered Igdrasil.

Thoughtful there sat Wisdom's son,
    Warder of the Well
    In whose waters dwell

Future, past and present lore,
From which Nornir evermore
Deeply drank.   He, knowing One,
Whene'er the early dawn was breaking,
And Jötunheim from sleep awaking,
His constant thirst these waters slaking,
    Would his very heart-strings steep
    In full horn drawn from the deep.

With silv'ry beard which far below
His girdle fell in glist'ning flow,
With wrinkled brow yet flashing eye,
Sat Bragi old, stern Mimir nigh,
He, worthy son of Odin high,
Who held the gift of minstrelsy.
    When, sudden, from the sacred Well
    Up would light foam and vapor swell,
        Or when o'erlapping wave,
        Springing from deepest cave,
        Outflung its misty spray,
    Then to his golden harp would stray
His quiv'ring hand, and forth would roll
Such strains as straight enchant the soul
And hold, spell-bound, the listener's ear

Rich runic rhymes
Of olden times,
High words of ancient lore,
Deep words from wisdom's store;—
While still thro' all the lofty measure,
With soft sounds breathing clear
Of Love's delight and godlike pleasure,
Were mingled notes of woe,
Tho' sadly, sweetly low,
The burden, wierd, unearthly wailing,
As tho' doomed spirits, unavailing,
Lost raptures mourned; then tones faint failing
Would rise again, with harp high sounding,
Thro' all the silent air resounding,
And louder, longer e'er swelled high,
Inspiring themes of poesy,—
Deeds of the gods that yet should be,
And deeds that were of Eld.
By Bragi's deep-rune-written tongue
Oft were such magic song-notes sung;
Oft with his harp, in vesture white,
He would the Æsir proud delight,
For Inspiration's power he held

Hither came the awful Vala,
Seeress from the land of Hela,
    Counsel wise to take;
    Here her thirst would slake.
Often, too, came Æsir hither;
Often sent the Jötuns whither
  Welled the fount of Wisdom fast,
Draining deep the horn of Knowledge
  Solving secrets of the Past.
Vapors, rising from the Well's edge,
  Shadows of the Future cast.

Now, great Odin, just and true,
God of gods, on Asgard's hill,
Tho' his ravens faithful flew,
Bringing news from all earth through,
Tho' he quaffed from Urda's bowl
Wisdom's draughts that feast the soul,
Tho' by Sökvabek he stayed
With fair Saga, all-wise maid,—
    Knowledge still
Lacked the God to right the ill.

Anxious, troubled, full of thought
To undo the evils wrought,

Gloomy, grieving,
　　Great God Odin
Uprising from Valhalla's throne,
Slow, the pillared Feast Hall leaving,
Engraven deep with runes within,
Sad, parting from those halls of light,
Forth rode he out into the night,
Down to dark Jötunheim alone.

　　Rode he long and rode he fast.
　　First, beneath the great Life Tree,
　　At the sacred Spring, sought he
　　Urdar, Norna of the Past;
　　But her backward seeing eye
　　Could no knowledge now supply.
Across Verdandi's page there fell
Dark shades that ever woes foretell;
The shadows which 'round Asgard hung
Their baleful darkness o'er it flung;
The secret was not written there
Might save Valhal, the pure and fair.
Last, youngest of the sisters three,
Skuld, Norna of Futurity,
Implored to speak, stood silent by,—

Averted was her tearful eye.
And now, deprived of guiding light,
Onward rode Odin thro' the night.

When to the Fountain's brink he came,
The God invoked the Sage's name.
   Arising slow
   Respect to show
To Odin great, the Æsir chief,
   Stood Mimir wise,
   Whose piercing eyes
Saw that the Father sought relief
From some sharp trouble, fear or grief.

Straight to him, then, Al-father spoke,
With questioning words the silence broke
   " Oh ! all wise Mimir !
   Sprung of the Æsir,
  Wise wert thou e'er of old,
  Prophet and seer ! unfold
What mysteries the Fates may hold !
   Darkened Valhalla's hall,
   The gods, confounded all !
Shame and disgrace o'er Asgard's race

Hang like an evil shrouding pall.
Where is our perfect quiet gone?
Why has the peace of Asgard flown?
Whence come the ills, the wrongs that fill
With strife and care our happy Hill?
Has yet a god wrought this disgrace?
Or springs it from the Jötun race?
 Speak thou! for thou cans't tell!
 Speak! Watcher o'er the Well!
 For, by the oath of gods,
 Whatever rich rewards
 Thou seek, they shall be thine;—
 Thou hast my pledge divine!"

Then spoke Mimir, stern and slow,
Filling high his golden horn,
While deep murmurings, muttered low,
Up from out the Well were borne,—
Surges of all-knowing Time,
Utt'ring faint their solemn chime:
" Odin, drink! this beaker drain!
Every drop a Fate shall be;
Spill not one! great God, in vain
Misty veil shall lift for thee.

Yet e'er these waters can be thine,
Sure pledge of payment must be mine
Not helmet bright, nor corslet strong,
For they to war and strife belong ;
No jewels rare, nor golden store ;
Thine eye in pledge leave evermore."

"Uneven sway thy scales.
Blind meekness ever fails
To balance crafty strength,—
The strength that springs from ill
Behold ! at length
From guile and lies
Pure peace e'er flies.
Strength is evil, vain is will,
Meekness, weakness,—each is sin
While false Loki's brood within
Ye shall cherish and shall nourish,
Giving thus ill deeds to flourish.
Be Loki's brood outcast,
In deepest depths chained fast ;
Else on the cow'ring world
Shall torments fierce be hurled !
Ruined shall fall proud Asgard's wall,

Void be each throne,—guestless each hall !
Thro' the Serpent, Hel, and Fenrir
Shall come destruction, deep and drear.
But, battle with them as ye will,
Dread Ragnarock thro' them comes still.
Too long has Loki dwelt within,
Too long have Æsir cherished sin ;
Too late ! too late, great God ! too late !
Unchangeable the words of Fate.
Ward off the ills, if so ye may,—
But Ragnarock ye *cannot* stay !

  On Baldur's brilliant crest
  What shining glories rest !
   White vestured God !
   Love is his sword,
  Peace is his battle-cry !

But even now false Loki waits
Within the shade of Asgard's gates ;
Lo ! even now the Tempter stands
By Hœdur blind, with guiding hands.
  The hour is drawing nigh !
Alas ! full soon shall Asgard's light
Be quenched and lost in blackest night !

Then triumphs Loki base !
Ravens his fearful race !
Terrible shall be the hour
When is loosed their baleful power !
Thee, thee shall hideous Fenrir slay
With cruel fangs that awful Day
When Earth shall burn, gods pass away
All this great Friga knoweth well,
But heron's crown forbids to tell,—
The plumēd crown, Forgetfulness,
Condemns her lips to silentness.

"Quaff once again, O God !
But mark thou well each word.
Not strength of Thor, or heart of Tyr,
'Gainst Serpent, Hel, or fierce Fenrir,
Can aught alone.   Let all Æsir
Rise in their might, cast out to night
Loki's foul brood ; then, in the light
Of Justice high, let judgment fall
With equal measure upon all.
Restored Valhalla's purity,
Thus Ragnarock delayed may be.

Return thou, Odin, e'er too late !
Hear, and obey the words of Fate."

So ended Mimir, while the swell
Of sigh-like murmurs from the well
Ceased with his voice ; then all was still.
Back Odin rode to Asgard's Hill,
Where, in Valhalla's shield-hung hall,
Assembled were the Æsir all
To learn what might from Fate befall.
Again, when early dawn was breaking,
And Jötunheim from sleep awaking,
Then Mimir, in the morn's first glowing,
Going to the fountain's edge,
Drank ever of the clear mead flowing
In his horn, o'er Odin's pledge.

PART SIXTH.

CASTING OUT OF LOKI'S BROOD.

DEEP down in the realms of night,
    Hideous powers dwelt in might,
    Brought forth on the dragon's bed,*
    With dwarf's dew* and venom fed ;
Awful, dreadful shapes of terror,
Guilty forms of darkest horror !
    Demon birth,
    Accursed of Earth !
Well do the Æsir know the sight.
The traitor Loki was their father
By Angurboda, Jötun mother ;

* Dragon's bed and Dwarf's dew, are personifications of gold.

Fierce hate and wrong
With time grown strong;
The brood triumphant,
In this exultant,
By Fate 'twas given
That they should raven
Proud Asgard's sons and men among.

Seated high among the Æsir,
    In Valhalla's shield-hung Hall,
Words of judgment spake God Odin,
    Counsel took he with them all.
Fiercely burned the gods' just ire!
    Angry-browed, with shoulders bent,
    On their rune-graved staves they lent;
Thro' Loki's art, had peace within
Been slain, while loathsome forms of sin,—
The Wolf, the Serpent, and pale Hel,—
Permitted upon Earth to dwell.

Rising from his Judgment-Seat,
From his spear-supported Throne,
Tow'ring to his fullest height,
Spake great Odin, "Thou most fleet

Tried Hermodur! quick begone!
Bear my mandate! speed thou forth
Thro' the wild and frozen North;
From drear Jötun lands of night
Bring the foul death-dealing blight
To be judged by Æsir might."

'Twas done.   The deadly brood
Before the high Throne stood.
Wildly striving,
Wrestling, writhing,
Unwilling, to the Judgment came,
Compelled by power of Odin's name.
Defiant, haughty Loki reared
His lofty head; with threat'nings dared
Affront the gods; if so they feared
His power of ill, to cease from wrath,
Resign to him his race of death!
Bold Tyr, undaunted, smote swift blow
Then hurled the Evil One below.

With venom-dripping crest,
Fierce tail in mad unrest,
Coiling his loathsome length,

Launching forth rings of strength,
Forked tongue, and poisoned breath,
The Serpent, child of Death,
Menāced Valhalla high;
  With heaving throes,
  And deaf'ning blows,
Lashing the very sky.

Close by the Throne now Hela stood
Whose awful aspect chilled the blood;
  Gaunt and pallid,
  Grim and livid,
A frightful, ghastly shape was she,
As dead among the dead shall be.
Red lightnings flashed from hollow eyes,
Her dark robes gave forth groans and sighs.
Back shrank the Æsir, pale, aghast,
As thro' their midst the Dread One passed,
All reeking with the fumes of death,
Mad, drunken, wild with frantic wrath;
Malignant glared she round the Hall,
As, baleful, would she crush them all;
Shaking in rage her mighty arm,
Burning to work high Asgard harm.

Then thronēd Justice, roused at length
Seized each the monsters in his grasp,
Awful in ire and wondrous strength ;
In vain they strove 'gainst Odin's clasp
   Swiftly impelled thro' air
        In breathless race
        They flew thro' space,
        Thro' mist and cloud,
        With howlings loud.
   Cowered the Earth in fear !
While, in Valhalla, at the sight,
Shivered the Gods with faces white.

Into mid-ocean's dark depths hurled,
Grown with each day to giant size,
The Serpent soon enclosed the world,
With tail in mouth, in circle-wise ;
        Held harmless still
        By Odin's will,
With lurid eye, in strong despair,
        Belching forth fierce
        Winds that should pierce
With rain and storm, the trembling air.
        Up maëlstroms broke,

While thunders woke
With sullen roar,
From shore to shore,
As he, with baffled ire,
Writhed still in vain desire.

By Odin strong,
Avenging wrong,
In ice-bound realms of Niflheim dread,
In gloomy regions of the Dead,
Was hideous Hel
Condemned to dwell.
Hither, to her dark domain,
Came those worthless spirits, slain
By old age, disease, or pain,
Captive, by the Dragon, Death,
Borne on black-hued wings beneath ;
Unmarked by hero-gore,
There wade they evermore
In venom-streams that pour
'Round that dismal habitation ;
All restless driven
Till chains be riven
In the Day of consternation ;

When will those rigid bands
Rush forth from Hela's lands,
    And, in the shock
    Of Ragnarock,
Thro' Thund's roaring river,
Against the high Æsir,
  'Gainst the Einheriar,
  Led by Valkyriar,
  Shall strive that fearful host,
  The armies of the lost.

Elvidner was Hela's hall,
Iron-barred; with massive wall ;
Horrible that palace tall !
Hunger was her table bare ;
Waste, her knife ; her bed, sharp care
Burning Anguish spread her feast ;
Bleachēd bones arrayed each guest ;
Plague and Famine sang their runes,
Mingled with Despair's harsh tunes.
Misery and Agony
E'er in Hel's abode shall be !
'Round about Thund's torrent poured
Loud without, Garm, Hell-dog, roared

His howlings oft
Shook earth and main ;
Struggles all vain !
There lies he fast
Till time be past,
And Ragnarock burst forth at last.

In vain, alas ! did vengeance come ;
Doomed, even then, Valhalla's dome
Too late, too late !
Decrees of Fate,
Unchanged and sure,
Must still endure.
Stern Destiny, who can avoid ?
She, pitiless, shall govern all !
Fair Asgard's gold-thatched roofs must fall
Void be her thrones ; guestless each hall.
Alas ! the hour still came apace
When all of earth and Odin's race
In Ragnarock should be destroyed.

While, on the bridge of glass,
To take from whom might pass
 The toll of blood,
 Grim Modgud stood;
 There, Hel shall reign
 Till, freed from chain,
In Ragnarock she rave in strife,—
Evil 'gainst Good, and Death 'gainst Life.

Remained for doom Fenrir alone;
Even Al-father on his throne
Trembled before that Jötun power,
Fearing should come the woeful hour,
 Decreed by Nornir,
 Foretold by Mimir,
 To most high Æsir,
When bright Valhal be plunged in gloom,
The Wolf's red jaws be Odin's tomb.

Exultant in his awful strength
Before the gods he stood at length.
 None but brave Tyr might dare
 To come the Wolf anear.
Twice did the Æsir strive to bind.

Twice did they fetters powerless find ;
Iron or brass of no avail,
Naught, save thro' magic could prevail.

　　　Gleipnir, at last,
　　　By Dark Elves cast,
In Svartalf-heim, with strong spells wrought
To Odin was by Skirnir brought.
As soft as silk, as light as air,
Yet still of magic power most rare ;
Wound round his limbs in weblike fold,
Full tight did Gleipnir Fenrir hold.

　　　Striving in vain
　　　Freedom to gain,
Each struggle only tighter bound ;
The Wolf lay chainēd on the ground.
With bristling back and gnashing teeth,
The monster rolled the throne beneath ;

　　　The venom froth
　　　From gory mouth
Was scattered by his blistering breath ;
Ever he sought in rage to rise,
Drawn ever back by magic plies ;

　　　With frenzied bite
　　　And furious might,

Would tear apart his fetters light.
          Mad howlings loud
          Pierced Asgard proud;
          More frantic grew!
          His huge weight threw
          From side to side;
          His hideous hide
          With dust and gore
          Was covered o'er.
          With foaming jaws
          And outstretched claws
Then glared he, impotent, about;
With fury heard the taunting shout,
The shrill laughter of the Æsir,
Derision loud of all save Tyr,
Thro' him one-handed evermore.

          Bound firm, this scourge o'
          Fierce Loki's fiercer bi
               On rocky isle
               To wait th
     A sword betwee
     The mighty
     On earth

PART SEVENTH.

THOR AND THE DAUGHTERS OF ÆGIR.

ON their azure pillows lying,
 O'er them distant murmurs dying,
 Ocean caves beneath replying
  From mermaid's horn
  To echoes borne
  On winged breeze
  O'er land and seas
From Asgard, Midgard, Jötunheim.
 Gently rocking to and fro,
 Ægir's daughters ceaseless go ;
 Mantles blue the maidens wear,
 Snow-white bosoms gleaming bare,

Sea-grass green their floating hair,
Still onward rolling, keeping time.

Who so fair as the waves,
Ægir's daughters,
Dancing waters!
Lapping lightly on the land,
Sporting softly on the strand,
Chasing one another.
Then the breeze, their brother,
Ruffles their crests,
Scatters their spray,
While their billowy breasts,
Heaving high in their play,
Swell and throb! In coral caves
Reigns King Ægir,
Feasts the Æsir,
Feasts he, too, the drownĕd Ones
Hither brought by Ran, his queen,
Swathed in shrouds of sea-weed green,
Fringed with shells; while still the sheen
Of pallid limbs and whit'ning bones,
E'er ghastly through the meshes comes
Of the net, in which each day

Unwary sailors catches she,
Grim Sea King's guests below to be.

Who so fierce as the waves,
When, from deep ocean caves,
Ægir shall call,
Shall summon all
To bear his fury on high!
Madly raging, roaring, lashing,
'Gainst steep crags in wild wrath crashing,
Up to Heav'n their spray-clouds dashing,
Mingling sea and sky!

Hither comes Thor,
The Thunderer,
To sport with those maids at rest.
Sleepily lies each maiden calm,
Gently drifting, with snow-white arm
Folded on billowy breast;
Foam-wreaths over the floating hair,
Swelling surges murmuring e'er
Lullaby songs that soothe to rest.

But fierce Thor,
The Thunderer.

Loves no calm !
Peace has no charm
To lull his soul to rest.
Comes he hither to sport an hour.
In Jötun's land,
With mighty hand,
His Æsir power
Rang in the rock
In tempest shock,
And raised dread fear in giant's breast.
What Odin sought,
That strong Thor wrought ;
And, now returned,
For sport he burned
E'er yet he reached Bilskirnir's bower.

From their rest the maids are waking,
Dimpling smiles o'er soft cheeks breaking
Sparkling showers from fingers shaking,—
Foamy fingers, light and fair ;
While bright Day from car of gold
Scatters gems of price untold
To bedeck each virgin rare.
Clinging, clasping in caresses,

To his breast the great God presses
Each soft maid, while floating tresses
    Wrap him in embraces cold.

    Burning Thor, with kisses fierce,
    Will their frozen bosoms pierce,
    Seizes in enfolding arms;
Filled with passion, strong desire,
Lustful flames e'er mounting higher,
    Presses wildly yielding forms,
    Riots on their sparkling charms.
Lightly still the maids caress him,
Closer to their bosoms press him;
    Strange regrets and vague alarms
    Wake too late! now, filled with storms
    Of wild wrath, they vainly try
    From his mighty arms to fly.
More gently does their lover Thor,
To lie at peace the maids implore;
But struggling, rising in their rage,
While all the ocean powers engage
To free them from the Thunderer,
        At length his wrath they rouse;
Then ends in strife the rude carouse.

Fiercely the billows strive,
Madly they toss and writhe,
'Neath towers of froth they hide ;
While all the ocean wide
Is lashed in boiling surge.
Ægir sits trembling on his throne,
For power to match with Thor is none.
Now, from their towers the maids emerge
Now, driven back by tempest scourge,
　　　Rough, wild waters !
　　　True Jötun daughters !
Roaring, wrestling, battling, writhing,
Evil powers 'gainst Æsir striving ;
Now, lost 'neath walls of foaming froth,
Now, darting swift high billows forth !
　　Blinded by the spray they pour,
　　Deafened by their sullen roar,
　　　Mighty Thor,
　　　The Thunderer,
Flashes lightnings, rolls his thunder,
Tears their billowy arms asunder,
Undoes their fiercely clinging clasp,
Upholds them firmly in his grasp,

Upholds them high
'Neath lowering sky,
Rampant raging, shrieking shrill,
Holds them powerless at his will;
Still the maidens higher lifts,
Dashes 'gainst the frowning cliffs,—
Dashes with his gathered strength !
His wrath appeased, he turns at length,
And muttering in his red beard low,
While glaring still from bended brow,
Home to Bilskirnir wends he slow;
With mocking laughter doth he go.

PART EIGHTH.

ODIN'S VISIT TO THE VÄLA.

OF all the gods of Asgard fair
    Who did in Valhal's feast-hall meet,
    'Mong Æsir twelve who gathered there
    To quaff their mead at Odin's feet,
And tell their tales of rare emprize
Beneath the light of Freya's eyes;—
Of all the twelve round Odin's throne,
Baldur, the Beautiful, alone,
The Sun-god, good, and pure, and bright,
Was loved by all, as all love light.

But now strange dreams and omens ill
    O'erclouded brows whence light e'er streamed;

While Midgard all, with Asgard's hill,
    Trembled for him, most cherished deemed.
At council grave did hither come
Beneath Valhalla's royal dome,
The anxious Æsir, thus to seek
What harm might hang o'er Baldur meek.

They prayed and offered great reward,
    And begged the Earth this charge to make,—
Round Baldur fair a watch and ward
    By day and night to ceaseless take.
Friga, his mother, restless went
To every plant, each element,
Each thing, with breath or breathless, she
Bound by an oath to harmless be
To her dear son; but, woe! ah, woe!
She passed the sacred mistletoe.

Then up rose Odin, anxious still,
    Saddled Sleipnir, of Löki's brood;—
To dark Niflheim, fearing some ill,
    Then quickly rode Al-Father good.
Forth in his path sprang Garm, the hound,
    Fierce keeper he of Hela's gate;

On rode Odin; from Earth came sound
    Of moaning over Baldur's fate.
Reached he soon the eastern portal
Whence returns no living mortal,
Chaunted loud the Saga's song-spell
Which shades shall call from death and hell.

Forth from the tomb the Väla came,
    Foreboding shape of woe and ill;
"What man art thou,—called by what name,—
    Who dares disturb my rest at will?
Dead have I lain long years gone by,
The snows of winter on me lie,
The rains have washed my bleached bones dry
    Long since the worms have ate their fill;
And now thou 'rt come to break my rest,—
Speak! I *must* answer thy behest!"

"Vegtam my name is, Valtam's son,
    And come I now to question thee;
Behold these seats! see every one
    Bedecked with rings and jewelry;
For whom prepared? The mead is set,
    The foaming draught with shield laid o'er;—

For whom the feast? the guest stays yet!
   Can gods withhold from Hela's shore?"

For Baldur gleams the beaker bright,
   His seat is set by Hela's side:
Compelled to speak by power of might,
   Silent henceforward I abide.
Hœdur, by Löki's fraud led on,
Blind arbiter of sighs and tears!
   Will slay the bright, the mighty One,
And bring the end on Odin's heirs.
   But, see! th' avenger, Vali, come,
Sprung from the west, in Rindus' womb,
True son of Odin! one day's birth!
He shall not stop nor stay on earth
His locks to comb, his hands to lave,
His frame to rest, should rest it crave,
Until his mission be complete,
And Baldur's death find vengeance meet."

Close not thy lips! I further seek
   The name of her who will not mourn,
Who will not weep for Baldur meek,
   But scornful smiles from eve till dawn."

"Thou art not Wegtam, as I deemed!
    Closed are my lips forever more."

"Nor art *thou* Väla, as thou seemed!
    No seeress thou of Hela's shore,
But mother of the giants dread,
Appointed guarders of the dead!"

"Ride on, great Odin! thou hast found
    Answers to all that troubled thee;
I to my cold sleep under ground,
    Will lay me calm and quietly.
Compelled, unwilling, have I said;
My words shall weigh on thee as lead.
Never for man shall ope my tomb
Till fatal Ragnarock be come!"

So homeward thro' dark Hela's shade
Odin his upward journey made;
Passed close beside the waters still
That lave the roots of Igdrasil;
Nor heeded Valkyr's greetings fair,
When now he reached the purer air;
That air to him breathed but one sigh
"Baldur the Beautiful must die!"

BALDUR'S DEATH.

With mournful brow and heavy eye,
  Came Odin to Valhalla's gate,
And passed the fateful Nornir by,
  But found within all joyful state;
For Æsir strong and Vingolf fair
Had met in Baldur's honor there,
And placed him in their midst on high,—
A mark for spear and archery;
Most god-like of the gods was he,
And proven deathless now to be.

Huge rocks and mighty boulders Thor
  Hurled with full force, but without harm;
And Vidar, with the Thunderer,—
  And Njörd,—the Sun-god bore a charm!
Loki alone stood silent by;
Mad, jealous hate was in his eye;
Swift his device,—as ancient dame,
He to the loving Mother came,
And thro' fair words the secret found,—
That all in, on, above the ground,
Except the feeble mistletoe,
Had sworn to shield her son from woe.

Then loud laughed Loki! swift returned,
  The slighted plant within his hand,
Soon the blind Hœdur he discerned;
  Then, giving him the tender wand,—
"Wherefore, O Hœdur! dost not pay
Due honor to this festal day?
Dost thou not see the Æsir great
Think it not ill to show him state?
Blind as thou art, I'll lead to where
Bright Baldur stands, a target fair;
Thou knowest well, Creation now
To work no ill has taken vow."

Blind Hœdur threw,—ah, woe! the dart
  By Loki from the frail plant shred,
Pierced fatal to the Sun-god's heart.
  Baldur the Beautiful lay dead!

Dead lay the Sun-god. Never more
  Should summer-light stream from his brow
To do him honor, to the shore
  Came Odin, with the Æsir now;
Heroic souls, by Valkyr led,
Ljus-Alfers, Vans, thro' sorrow sped

To swell the train that mourned the dead.
Near, with bent brows, the Thunderer stood;
While Hœdur, bowed 'neath weight of blood,
All shod with silence, slow drew near
To weep with him their brother dear.

On swift Hringhorni's giant prow
  Baldur the Beautiful they laid,—
The burning ship must bear him now
  Thro' gloomy skies of gathering shade;
Dull yellow fringe on pale gold shroud
Gleamed coldly 'neath the wintry cloud.
Then Odin lit the funeral pyre,—
Out to the north, in streams of fire,
To Saga's call his spirit sailed,
While Nature's heart his loss bewailed.
Ne'er shall the mild god hasten home
Till fatal Ragnarock be come.

HERMODUR'S VISIT TO HELA.

Sad Mother! watching her dear son
  Borne by the burning ship away,

Dreamed might be Loki's work undone
  Should she to Hela ransom pay.
With veilēd head and mournful brow,
Then did she to the Æsir go,
And sought which of them all would prove
The depth and greatness of his love,
By riding swift to Elvidnir,
Ransom from Hel the White-God dear,
And bring him back, the loved of all,
Safe to his seat in Asgard's hall.

At once Hermodur claimed the quest,
  Mounted Sleipnir, who saddled stood,
And never sought he stay nor rest
  Till he nine days had been on road;
Then, on the tenth, he came to where
The bridge of glass hung on a hair
Thrown o'er the river terrible,—
The Giöll, boundary of Hel.
Now here the maiden, Mödgud, stood
Waiting to take the toll of blood,—
A maiden horrible to sight,
  Fleshless, with shroud and pall bedight.

As swift Hermodur thundered by,—
  "Stop!" quoth the maiden, "give thy name
Thou hast not hue of those who die;
  Only yestreen five dead troops came,
Yet trembled not this bridge so much
Beneath their tread as thy one touch."

And when he asked, "Did Baldur ride
  Down to the dead within her sight?"
"E'en now," she answered, "at the side
  Of Hel he feasts in halls of night."
On rode Hermodur.   Fearful Garm,
The Hel-dog, bayed, nor caused alarm;
The Nornir dread, by Igdrasil,
Could not withstay him 'gainst his will.
So he to dark Elvidnir came,
And there invoked Hel's mighty name,—
Gave Friga's message, told her how
All nature mourned for Baldur now,
And prayed her set the White-god free,
That joy in Asgard's halls might be.

"And is it so?" swift answered Hel;
  "Now shall the truth of this appear!

If all things loved thy God so well
   No loss of Baldur need thou fear.
Let all things from fair Nature's birth,
Breathing or breathless, on the earth,
For him, throughout creation, mourn;
And then your Sun-God shall return."

Back rode Hermodur to the hall
   Where Friga and the Æsir stayed;
There, filled with hope, he told them all
   What promises dark Hela made.
Already light seemed to return,
For did not Nature e'en now mourn?
What breathing thing, or without breath,
That would not mourn for Baldur's death?

Quick o'er the earth great Friga sent
   Her mandate that all things should weep
And gods and Vanir loving lent
   Their powerful aid, that all should keep
A day of universal woe
   To ransom Baldur from below.

Now, as Hermodur homeward rode
   From bearing Friga's message forth,

A giantess, all shameless, strode
   From a dark cave that fronts the north.
Veilless her head, undimmed her eye,
A hateful smile her lips shone nigh;—
'Twas Loki, in the form of Thökt,
Who, evil, at the summons mocked.
" If so thou please, let Nature wail;
Without *my* tears 'twill not avail.
Why should *I* weep, whose heart is dry?
Weeping and wailing, none will I !
Living or lifeless, ill or well,
Let Baldur bide his time with Hel !"
Then, with loud laughter, Thökt was gone,
But where she stood a stream poured down.

Hermodur sad returned, and slow,—
Through Asgard spread the words of woe,
Baldur the Beautiful shall ne'er
From Hel return to upper air !
Betrayed by Löki, *twice* betrayed,
The prisoner of Death is made ;
Ne'er shall he 'scape the place of doom
Till fatal Ragnarock be come !"

PART NINTH.

KING ÆGIR'S FEAST.

NOW Loki's last, worst work was done.
Triumphant Wrong, exalted high,
O'ershadowed even Odin's throne,
And dimmed the glow o'er Earth and
sky.
Weeping and gloom
Fill'd Valhal's dome;
The stars gleamed pale
Thro' Heaven's cloud-veil;
Fair Day reined back his steed of light,
Exultant rode forth Jötun Night;
Lost in the consciousness of woe,
All purposeless the Æsir go.

Withered the Earth!
Creation's birth
Reeled blindly 'neath the staggering blow.
Baldur, defenceless, innocent,
Naught but his shining purity
'Gainst evil deeds as surety,
To Hela's feast by craft was sent.

Evil before,
Now more and more
Evil and base the traitor grew ;
Lower and lower fell he ever,
Only for ill his each endeavor;
Fled from his heart the pure and true ;
A reckless raging
Each power engaging,
Until to all his very name
Symbol of craft and hate became ;
While, still defiant, held he high
His haughty head, 'neath lowering sky.
Yet still, tho' lost, upon his face
At times a grace
Faint glimmered of the ancient day
When he and Odin. one in soul,

Mingled their love in flowing bowl ;
A transient gleam,—a semblance cast
By shad'wy mem'ries of the past,—
    Arising dim to fade away.

Now, to assuage the high gods' grief
And bring their mourning some relief,
        From coral caves
        'Neath ocean waves,
      Mighty King Ægir
      Invited the Æsir
        To festival
        In Hlesey's hall;
That, tho' for Baldur, every guest
        Was grieving yet,
        He might forget
Awhile his woe in friendly feast.

The vexed waves heard the summons given;
From white lips hissed their wrath to Heaven
    Who joy or feasting e'er should know
    While Baldur sat with Hel below?
    Panting, heaving, restless waters!
    Sobbing, moaning, Ægir's daughters!

Bellowing in sullen roar,
Beating on the rock-girt shore,
Tumbling wild in dismal tide,
Whit'ning all the deep sea wide,
The booming surges thundering fell
O'er sunken rocks in hoarse, sad swell,
While the thick mists flaunted high
Funēral banners to the sky.
Weeping waters !
Ægir's daughters,
Unforgetful,
And regretful,
Wailing over Baldur's fate;
While far below
Their mournful flow,
On throne of state
Sat King Ægir,
Who the Æsir
Would feast at banquet rarely great.

Beneath the watery dome,
With crystalline splendor,
In radiant grandeur,
Upreared the sea-god's home.

More dazzling than foam of the waves,
E'er glimmered and gleamed thro' deep caves
The glistēning sands of its floor,
Like some placid lake rippled o'er.
    Lights opalescent
    Glowed phosphorescent
Thro' its sparkling emērald walls ;
    Flowers the fairest,
    Rich treasures rarest,
Lavish decked its billōwy halls;
    Bright shells from ocean's bed,
    Gem-like, their luster shed,
        Twinkling in rays most bright,
            Mingled their gleaming
            Brilliantly beaming
            Rainbow-like light.

    Myriad things of ocean,
    With soft gliding motion,
    Through branched coral grove
    Would dartingly rove,
Thro' blooms and o'er palm trees,
    'Mid mosses and sea-fan,
Swayed by the cool breeze

In the grottoes of Ran.
While thro' crystal gulfs were gleaming
Ocean depths, with wonders teeming;
  Shapes of terror, huge, unsightly,
Loomed thro' vaulted roof translucent;
  Silver finnēd fish swam lightly,
  Sparkling showers scatt'ring brightly, —
Phosphorescent rays pelucent.

Devouring Ran, by Ægir's side,
Smiled, treacherous, thro' the feast-hall wide.
  In festive state awaited they
  Their Æsir guests to deep Hlesey.
At length a conch-shell, hung on high,
      Rang hoarse and loud,
      A greeting proud,
As Odin and his numerous train
      To hall drew nigh;
While Heimdal, with great Gjallar-horn,
Answered the notes, on ripples borne,
      In clear refrain.

Then Vans and Æsir, mighty gods,
Of Earth, and air, and Asgard, lords—

Advancing with each goddess fair,
A brilliant retinue most rare.—
    Attending mighty Odin, swept
      Up wave-worn aisle in radiant march,
Thro' pillared crystals, glittering bright,
Fair diamond lamps, dispersing light.
    Around them briny breezes crept,
        Wafting them on
        To Ægir's throne
      'Neath billowy arch,
Where fountains flowing, filled with mead,
And goblets wreathed with bright sea-weed
        For them abounded ;
        While songs resounded
        Loud and high
        In welcoming cry,
As near and nearer, drew they nigh.

With burnished gold helm, at their head
Great Odin up the feast-hall led,—
Mighty father of the Æsir !
With his bride, the blue-eyed Friga ;
Azure robes around her flowing,
        Heron-crested.

Snow-white breasted,
Love upon her soft lips glowing
For her lord,—her heart's desire.

Freya close beside was treading,
Dazzling rays around her shedding
From the starry wreath of light,—
Sun-worlds,—glowing scarce so bright
As fair Beauty's lovely queen
Hast'ning on thro' crystal sheen.

Sweet Bragi, Njörd, Forseti mild,
And gold-curled Sif, the spouse of Thor,
With Vidar, Frey, and many more,
Up thro' the central nave defiled;
Absent alone the Thunderer.
As close to Ægir's throne they drew,
With ev'ry step the conches blew;
The shrill notes rang,
And skoal loud sang !
Skoal to each guest
At Ægir's feast.

Higher and louder swelled the glee,
Merrier the festivity !

When, suddenly, in shadow fell
   A shade from Hel
   The hall within;
   A figure tall
Crept in by stealth,—a shape of sin
'Twas Loki reared his hateful form;
   Like lull in storm,
A dismal silence shrouded all,
And ended the high festival.

PART TENTH.

LOKI'S PUNISHMENT.

ALONE, forlorn,
    Apart withdrawn,
    An outcast, Loki leant
'Gainst coral feast-seat in the aisle;
    On traitor shameless each the while
    Reproachful glances bent.

" Now, wherefore art thou hither come,
An unsought guest, in Ægir's home?
    At festival
    In banquet hall,
For thee, behold! no seat is set;
No flowing mead thy lips shall wet.

Depart ! thou scourge of Asgard's race
Among the gods *thou* hast no place."

'Twas Bragi spoke;
From Loki broke
Resounding words of insult vile;
" Confusion on all
Within this hall !
Death to the Æsir !
Ruin to Ægir !
May flames of Surtur
Destroy ye all !
Empty your pleasures,
Worthless your treasures ;
In a brief while
Cometh your fall.
Even now Hela
Glares at Valhalla !
Never, ye gods ! again
Shall meet your festive train
At banquet high.
Lo ! darkened sky
Attests my power.
In woeful hour

Your Baldur fell thro' subtle art ;
        I plucked the dart
That, surely, pierced the Sun-God's heart.
        When Nature wept,
        As Thökt, I kept
My tearless watch, lest he
From Hela's kingdom freed might be.
        From earliest dawn
        Of Time's young morn,
        On Asgard's hill,
        My steadfast will
Opposed you in each high endeavor ;
        Fair tho' I seemed,—
        Friend, as *ye* deemed,—
A double game I played you ever.
Triumphant, tho' I now give way ;
        The stronger ye
        This time may be.
Soon, Æsir ! comes the woeful day !
Dread Ragnarock ye none can stay ;
Then my fierce power shall Valhal know,
And Asgard feel me open foe.

"Tremble, ye Æsir !
And you, King Ægir !
Hark how fierce Fenrir
Howls loud and long !
  Now, Odin ! speed
Valkyriar,
Your maids of war;
For in Valhalla
  Soon is there need
Of brave and strong
  Einheriar !

"Ye fair-faced goddesses ! Not one
By Beauty's light or Wisdom's ray,
    Can turn away
  The woe begun.
  Soon, ravening, shall
  Thro' proud Valhal,
  And bright Vingolf,
  Rage the Gray Wolf !
No seat have *I*, as welcome guest,
    At this your feast !
  Where horrors dwell
  In halls of Hel.

Behold ! a mightier feast is spread,—
    Meats that nourish,
    And cause to flourish
The ghastly armies of the Dead.
Above, loud crows your golden Cock !
    Once hath the sound
    Echoed around !
The third time heralds Ragnarock !"

Scoffing he spoke, and sneering gazed
On throng assembled;—mute, amazed,
They, listening, stood an instant's space.
    Then wrath swelled high,
    Darkened each eye,
    Convulsed each face !
    Stung by insulting taunt,
    Enraged at odious vaunt,
Quick to his feet each, furious, sprang;
Thro' dome and arch deep curses rang !
When, suddenly, a peal of thunder
Shivered the crystal gulfs asunder;
With lurid ray, fierce lightnings played,
    Reflected bright
    In diamond light,

'Gainst billowy wall
     Of banquet hall,
While winds and waves loud tumult made
Then quaked the undulating floor,
     Quivered each amber lamp,
     Each wreath of sea-weed damp;
     Rocked the translucent dome;
     Deep aisles were flecked with foam
It was the mighty Thunderer, Thor!

     Swift drawing nigh
     With flashing eye
     And flaming beard,
     Wroth, mutt'ring low
     'Neath bended brow,
He raised great Mjölnir high;
On traitor vile he glared.
     Before the dread
     Avenger's tread
     Back Loki shrank,
     'Mid steel swords' clank,
And, craven! trembling fled!

Mad for vengeance, wild with hate,
Forth the gods, infuriate,

From gay halls in coral caves,
Rushed thro' surging, swelling waves !
  In fearful race,
  To Loki chase
  The wrathful Æsir gave !
Now, thro' boiling whirlpools darting,
Hissing depths, asunder parting;
Now, the foaming billows breasting,
Never for a moment resting ;
Until, wearied out at length,
Gathering all his failing strength
   Himself to save,
The traitor, to a salmon changing,—
   Slipping, sliding,
   Doubling, gliding,
Beneath a roaring cascade ranging,
  Halted for an instant's space.

In that instant's pause for breathing,—
Waters 'round him frothing, seething,
Sides with fear and flight fast heaving,—
His fierce enemies perceiving
Golden scales thro' foam-clouds flashing,
   On him dashing,

Seized and bound him, firmly lashing
    Struggling form with horrid coils
    Fettered by the entrails torn
    From his own son, Jötun-born,
      Laid he, hopeless, in the toils;
While the Æsir, mocking, taunting,
Chained him—powèrless and panting,—
Fast to a triple-pointed rock,
Till freed by final battle-shock.
Ere they left him in his anguish,
O'er his treacherous brow ungrateful,
Skadi hung a serpent hateful,
Venom-drops for aye distilling,
Every nerve with torment filling;
Thus shall he in horror languish.

By him, still unwearied kneeling,
  Sigyn at his tortured side,—
Faithful wife! with beaker stealing
  Drops of venom as they fall,—
  Agonizing poison all!
Sleepless, changeless, ever dealing
  Comfort, will she still abide;
Only when the cup's o'erflowing

Must fresh pain and smarting cause,
Swift, to void the beaker going,
Shall she in her watching pause.
Then doth Loki
Loudly cry;
Shrieks of terror,
Groans of horror,
Breaking forth in thunder peals!
With his writhings scared Earth reels.
Trembling and quaking,
E'en high Heav'n shaking!
So wears he out his awful doom,
Until dread Ragnarock be come.

In this poem, Loki's final capture and punishment only is told.
Escaping from the banquet hall of Ægir, he fled to the mountains,
where he secreted himself until discovered by Odin, who, with the
rest of the Æsir, went in pursuit. Loki, to avoid capture, assumed
the form of a salmon, but was finally taken by Thor.

PART ELEVENTH.

RAGNAROCK.

'TWAS done! th' avenging deed was
            wrought!
        Alas, too late!
        Decrees of Fate
        With judgment fraught
        Must be obeyed.
        With Baldur dead
Pure Peace and Innocence had fled :
When his swift, shining course was stayed,
Then darkness gathered o'er the Earth,
Strife and Corruption sprang to birth.
Tho' Loki lay fast bound below,
            The seeds of woe

Were sown broadcast;
Nearer and nearer drew the hour,
Blacker and fiercer grew the power
That should o'erwhelm all things at last.

Grim Fimbul raged, and o'er the world
Tempestuous winds and snow-storms hurled;
The roaring ocean icebergs ground,
And flung its frozen foam around
E'en to the top of mountain height;
          No warming air,
          Nor radiance fair
Of gentle Summer's soft'ning light,
Tempered this dreadful glacial night.

Three other winters howled abroad
With furious storms of ice and hail;
Beneath the might of fearful gale
Earth trembled; while, thro' wild abyss,
The seas around, upthundering, roared
To sable skies, with moan and hiss!
Crag hurled on crag with deaf'ning crash;
Great Igdrasil, beneath the lash
Of tempest shock, all quivēring stood;

The blackened skies were flecked with blood
By raging powers of Darkness riven
From their fixed orbits in the heaven,
The pallid stars were ruthless driven
       Thro' flying cloud.
Hoarse earthquakes bellowed loud ;
Crumbled the rocks; forests down bowed !
Forth burst the hot volcanic stream ;
Flashed forth the fatal lightning's gleam ;
Streamed sheets of flame to lurid sky;
Devouring tongues of fire rose high,
Did mighty Igdrasil enshroud,
And Time expired in burning flood.

       All bonds were burst ;
       Troops of accursed
Tore rampant thro' the Earth and air ;
The gloomy hordes of Night roamed free;
The powers that erst from Chaos came—
Fire and Water, Darkness, Death—
'Gainst Earth and Asgard strove in wrath.
More fiercely than the lurid glare
Of conflagration, hideously
Shone on men's faces Murder's flame !

Brother slew brother—father, child ;
Men turned to tigers, mad for gore !
Creation raged ! war followed war ;
Impiety, Injustice piled
Huge heaps of horror to the sky ;
Passion, and Fear, and every crime
Mad riot held thro' this dread time—
Undaunted, reared their pale heads high !

So came, with blood and tempest shock,
  Wild Ragnarock !
  The Day of Doom—
  The hour was come !
Shrill crowed Valhalla's golden Cock !
The crimson bird of Hel replied.
Fierce Fenrir flung his fetters wide,
Deep howling, rushed with ravening jaws,
Nostrils flame flashing, outstretched claws,
Hot eyeballs glaring for his prey ;
On-leaping thro' the gulfs of air,
With jaws agape from Earth to Heaven,
A yawning chasm of red fear !
Well knew the Wolf, that awful Day,
What prey should to his maw be given.

In giant wrath, the Serpent tossed
In ocean depths, till, freed from chain,
He rose upon the foaming main ;
Beneath the lashings of his tail,
Seas, mountain high, swelled o'er the land ;
Then, darting mad the waves acrost,
Pouring forth bloody froth like hail,
Spurting with poisoned, venomed breath
Foul, deadly mists o'er all the Earth,
Thro' thundering surge, he sought the strand

Over the lurid ocean flew
The Death-ship, Nagelfari, dread,
Filled with Hrimthursar, led by Hrym,
Bearing huge rocks ; the winds that blew
And sped it on this final time,
Were dying sighs of mortal dead.

Now at the head of Hel's pale host,
Those livid armies of the lost,
The unchained Loki furious came.
Grimmer and closer, thro' the gloom
On pressed they to the plain of Doom.
Scorching on high, rolled pillared flame ;

With bayings that thro' Nature pierced,
From Gnipa, Garm, the Hel-Dog, burst;
 In mad, chaotic rout,
  Thro' baleful light,
  The powers of Night
 Reeled and careered about!

 Amid the hideous din,
  Confusion dire,
The blackened Heav'ns were rent in twain;
  Thro' the jaggēd rift,
  With dazzling radiance swift,
  Streamed the World of Fire!
  'Gainst the hosts of Sin,
On hastening to broad Vigrid's plain,
The blazing sons of Muspel rode;
'Thro' gloomy clouds their pathway glowed.
  Down thro' the fields of air,
  With glittering armor fair,
  In battle order bright,
  They sped, while seething flame
  From rapid hoof strokes came.
Leading his gleaming band, rode Surtur,
'Mid the red ranks of raging fire;

His very sword a ray of light
        Snatched from the Sun !
        Flinging on high
Flame banners flaunting to the sky,
Onward they came at headlong pace ;
The Rainbow Bridge, 'neath furious race,
Shivered and sank—its work was done !

        White as the winter snows,
        Great Heimdal now arose—
        Valhalla's Warder,
        High Heaven's Guarder !—
Siezed his huge trump and boldly blew.
Loudly and long thro' Asgard rang
Great Gjallar-horn, with startling clang !
That summons well the Æsir knew !
Then, for the third time, crowed the Cock
Assembling all for Ragnarock !

As thro' the Heavens the summons rang,
Swift to their Chief the Æsir sprang !
Fresh armor seized from steel-draped hall
Exulting loud in awful joy
That conflict mighty should employ

Once more their might,
E'en though the fight
Should end in Asgard's fatal fall;
For, high o'er Vigrid's gory plain,
The Æsir saw fair Gimli's fane.

Little delay was in that hour:
Great Odin gathered all his power!
Ah! well for him that to his feasts
Had bidden he such warrior guests.
Now, wakened by Valkyriar,
Brave armies of Einheriar
With stiffened fingers bound on swords;
With shield and lance,
'Mid bright spears' glance,
Pressed on amid the hastening gods.
Then, gold-helmed Odin at their head,
Valhalla's hosts to Vigrid led;
With polished armor shining bright,
And cuirass gleaming thro' the night,
On to the final battle sped.
Close by his side, the Thunderer.
With Odin, Fenrir closed in strife!
Awful and strong

That contest long,
For death and life !
Powerless to aid was mighty Thor ;
'Gainst *him* the fell World-Serpent raged,
And all his Æsir powers engaged !

Blood-stained the helmet's burnished gold
In struggles mad o'er Earth they rolled.
At last, huge Fenrir's wide-stretched jaw
Engulfed the God in grizzly maw;
Thus, by foul Loki's fearful son,
Was greatest ill to Asgard done.

Lo ! Vidar, as avenger, came
Of Odin's fame !
The Monster in his mighty grasp,
Resistless clasp,
He seized; loud howlings broke,
And far, affrighted echoes woke.
Upon his writhing foe
Planting his iron shoe,
Rending and tearing with vast strength,
Until, at length,
Split he Fenrir's jaws asunder !

The reft sky shook with deep death growls,
And sharp, prolongēd, hideous howls
Like harsh peals of angry thunder.
Scarce conquered was the Gray Wolf dread,
E'er, with the life blood oozing slow
From wound dealt forth by dying foe,
On Fenrir foul fell Vidar, dead.

    Caught in the loathsome toils
    Of Jormungandur's coils,
    Thro' all this fearful war
No aid could bear the Thunderer:
The Serpent, armed with fatal sting,
Loud clanking now with scaly side,
Fierce fold on fold out-lapping wide,
    With toss and fling
To crush the Æsir-champion tried.
      At length,
    With wondrous strength,
Great Thor the horrid coils off flung;
Beneath the blows of Mjölnir dread,
The savage Monster, stricken dead,
In jet-black gore lay weltering.
But, in that awful combat, stung

By venomed fang, nine steps and more
Back recoiled the unconquered Thor,
And in his last World-Victory died.

Once, high in Valhal held a god,
But now, a fallen shape abhorred,
        Condemned for ill
        Stern doom to fill,
Full long had Loki writhed enchained,
Tormented, tortured, agonized ;
    Stretched at gigantic length,
    Useless his Jötun strength,
Tearing at iron fetters fast ;
Heavings and howlings—all in vain !
There had he tossed long ages past,
Revolving schemes of deeds accursed,
Wild hopes of wrath and vengeance nursed
For these, alone, he freedom prized,
That, with his pristine power regained,
He hatred fierce might wreak at last ;
Joyful to him was Vigrid's plain.

Roused to fresh ire at Fenrir's fall,
Up-towered in rage his figure tall,

Breathing defiance deep and loud,
Leading ahead Hel's ghostly crowd,
With vengeful lust, the Æsir sought.
   Swift o'er the field,
   With brazen shield,
   And lance in rest,
Great Heimdal rushed to meet the foe
   'Mid streams of gore,
   While shout and roar
   And thund'rous blow
Convulsed the earth, the æther split ;
There, thro' the rift with flames alit,
Bright Muspel's sons in awful gaze,
One instant glaring in amaze,
Marked how in frenzied fight they fought.
Then, in death-struggle, wildly pressed,
Infuriate, grappling breast to breast,
In vengeful arms they, gasping, reeled.

  The universal fury swelled
   Fiercer on high !
   The vaulted sky,
   High arched with flame,
Resounded with the deaf'ning clang

Which, deep below, in earthquakes rang.
Millions advancing hosts repelled,
Whom millions met and fought, unquelled!
From air, and earth, and sea, there came
    Throngs until now in bondage held;
Down from their cloudy prisons swept
The sons of Ægir, fettered kept
By thunderbolt and lightning's chain.
From seething whirlpools of the main,
Up Ægir sprang with Ran's dank train
    Of pallid Drowned; while ravening waves
Huge, rearing high their foaming breasts,
Destruction bearing on their crests,
    To battle rushed from ocean caves.
Terrific conflict! each on field,
Alone, could devastation wield.
Host surged on host; then, rallying, flew
To join more fierce the strife anew.
            No thought of flight!
            On his own might
Each in this mad'ning hour relied.
Down to her very central point
Trembled the earth; thro' every joint
Of pale Creation's quiv'ring frame,

Confusion wild, and warring came :
  Till, darting down from scorching sky,
Great Surtur flung his fiery brand!
In conflagration flared the land,
  Shrivelled like scroll the heaven high;
    Above, below, surrounding fire
    Still mounting higher,
Played lurid 'gainst the crumbling home
Of Valhal's gods in Asgard's dome.

    Ended the frightful war.
    Alone, as conqueror,
    Stood Surtur, Victor!
  With ruined Nature's birth,
  Down sank the blackened Earth
    In boiling sea.
    All smould'ring fell!
That which from Chaos came,
 To Chaos back returned ;
    Disastrously,
In the eclipse of Asgard's lords,
Faded the twilight of the gods.
At length one universal fiame,
Enwrapping distant spheres, high burned;

Laid on one mighty funeral pyre,
Forth flashed in fierce consuming fire,
In World-blaze dread,—Earth, Heaven and Hell

PART TWELFTH.

REGENERATION.

SO Chaos wild again
    Reigned o'er Creation's fane.
    Foul Loki's brood had given birth
    To fear in Heav'n, and crime on Earth.
So deep had sunk corruption's stain,—
So far had spread dark sin and pain,—
        That Death alone
        Could e'er atone;
While thro' the flames of Surtur's sword
Alone could peace be yet restored.
When that dread World-blaze flared on high,
Mingling in ruin earth and sky,—

The lurid glow, still mounting higher,
Shone forth,—a god-sent purifier.

'Twas past.   The Fire-God's work was done.
        Died down the flame;
        Weak Nature's shame
Submerged in depths of shoreless sea;
The charrèd skies, the smoke-wreaths gray,
With battle's din, had passed away;
        Day had begun !
        All gloriously
Thro' Heaven's broad fields of trackless light
With splendors bursting thro' the night,
The fairer daughter of the Sun
Rode forth on her celestial way
        Round ether main,
    Where starry isles strew thick the plain;
        One dazzling blaze
        Of cloudless days
    Flooded all worlds with ecstacy.

        Triumphantly
Stept forth the High and Mighty One
    From mansions of Eternity,
Where rests for aye His golden throne;

To Whom Time was a moment's birth;
Strong with the strength of Heaven and Earth,
Victorious o'er sin and pain,
With wondrous majesty shall reign
In judgment's solemn panoply.

Then the Life-giving Spirit spoke;
            And sudden broke
Up from the bosom of the sea,
            Most beateously,
The vernal Earth, ambrosial;
Fair as the smile of new-born light,
And fairer far than when at dawn
Of young Creation's early morn,
Up-springing from chaotic night,
She sang her praise to proud Valhal.

Raising on high her forehead fair
Crowned with sweet flowers of beauty rare,
She smiled up to the crystal arch,
Laughing with fountain's gurgling plash,
And mountain streamlet's joyous dash;
            While shining planets far,
Moving in liquid harmony

Around the Throne of Him most High,
Pausing awhile in measured march,
Poured down a flood of softened beams,
Caught from blest Gimli's golden gleams,
      To greet their sister star.

Decked in bright robes of living green,
Enamelled o'er with flow'rets' sheen,
      Sweet Nature stood restored.
Ripe unsown harvests clothed the hills;
      The murmuring rills
Refreshing dews o'er meadows poured;
The mantling vines, luxurious, hung
With purple treasures richly fraught;
      While sunbeams wrought,
The leafy bowers of shade among,
A network rare of gold with dusk;
Wide gardens of sweet-smelling musk,
With jassamine and roses' scent,
To perfumed air more perfume lent;
Thick woods, whose boughs of fragrance flung
Their spicy odors to the breeze,
Rose in fresh coolness o'er the vale,
And gently swayed to balmy gale;

The bending trees,
With burnished fruit, were weighted deep:
    While, from the steep,
Rivers of joy rolled down each dale;
On the sweet breeze that gently swelled
From groves of cassia and of palm,
Forth tuneful voices gaily welled
From feathered songsters of the air,
Whose gorgeous plumes, in colors bright,
Flashed jewelled gleams of rainbow light,
Mingled with roseate sunbeams fair.
Caressing breaths of heavenly balm
Young Nature lapped in blessèd calm;
While throbbing pulses of the Earth
Beat high at her glad second birth.

    Thro' all that doomful Day
When Surtur's flames destroyed the world,
And back to Chaos Nature hurled,
    Two gentle beings lay
    Concealed in Mimir's wood—
Hodminir's forest deep;—unscathed,
Unshaken by the tempest shock,
In dreamless slumbers sweetly swathed,

They, all unharmed, passed 'neath the brand
That burning sword which o'er all waved,
Devouring else, air, sea, and land,—
Alone, of all Creation, saved
From that resistless fire and flood
Of Time-destroying Ragnarock.

Unconscious thro' that hideous strife,
Awakened now to blissful life,
Guileless and lovely, they arose
In new-born strength and purity.
All passion passed, with care and woes;
Calmed now convulsed Creation's throes
To peaceful rest and surity.
Thro' all that night of horror dread
On dews of morning they were fed;
Now, lifting up their joyful eyes
In rapturous wonder and surprise,
⠀⠀⠀⠀They gazed around
From ether vault to teeming ground.
Above, the broad horizon's zone
With orient effulgence shone;
Beneath, the bounteous Earth sent up
Unfading grass, and flow'ret's cup,

Filled with the wine of early dawn;
With dew-drops gemmed, each emerald blade
Within its gleaming, liquid light
The image of the heavens displayed;
Eternal spring breathed thro' the morn,
And cast o'er all her halo bright.

So beauteous lay,—so tranquilly,—
The virgin daughter of the sea,
That the two souls who on her gazed,
Themselves most innocent and fair,
All perfect 'mid perfection rare,
By myriad blooming charms amazed,
Received with joy this dwelling place.
High altars to the gods they reared,
Pure Gimli's fane they loved and feared ;
So, blest and happy, chosen were
As parents of a nobler race.

Upon the perfume-breathing plain
Of Idavöller, where before
Stood Asgard's gold-roofed halls of yore,
The joyous Æsir met again ;
Conquerors from awful fight,

Grown pure thro' fire, grown strong with strife
Passed thro' dread death to endless life,
As thro' dark bars to fane of light :
    For Loki's reign was o'er.
      No more
Should foul wrong, loathsome, side by side
With peace and purity abide.
    Broken the power of Hel ;
      Freed from her gloomy chain,
        Baldur again
Rose, luminous, from realms of night.
All shapes of Ill, as rolled away
The Twilight gloom before his ray,
Back to their bonds appallēd fell :
On Vigrid's plain all evil died.
    That great Atonement-Day,
In godlike love, thro' godlike might,
Led back the Æsir, purified,
To firmer thrones and brighter halls
Than e'er were found in Asgard's walls.
Love smiled thro' all the universe ;
Arm linked in arm, in sweet converse,
Baldur, with Hœdur seated nigh,
In perfect peace and harmony,

Glad greetings gave exultantly,
As up the heights to Ida's plain
The happy Æsir rose again,
In the clear dawn, triumphantly.

With crystal walls, gold-fretted roof,
A new-built Valhal, tempest-proof,
        Towered aloft ;
Without, within, all rich and rare,
Steel to make strong, and jewels fair
        All lavish spread
O'er pavement broad, and vaulted dome ;
        While music soft
Floated, full voiced, high overhead,
Guiding the Æsir to their home.
Again the beakers deep brimmed o'er ;
Again the great gods' wondrous lore
And mighty deeds of Eld were sung ;
        With runic rhyme
        Of earlier time
Again the pillared Feast-Hall rung.
But now no Battle-Maidens stood
Round Odin's Throne, at hero-feast,
With gory armor, shields of blood ;

All useless now Valkyriar,
War brought forth no Einheriar,
  For war had ceased.
High o'er young Earth and Ida's plain,
  By Gimli's fane—
Close by the Throne of Him Most High
With folded wings, stood Victory ;
While sweetly thro' each sounding sphere
In tones that swelled on waves of air,
He spoke, commanding " Peace ! "
Gave chains to Death—to Pain, surcease

Wide thrown, lo ! Gimli's golden gate
On most harmonious hinges swang,
As, from His Everlasting Seat,
Arrayed in majesty complete,
The Judge Eternal, glorious, came,
Weighing, supreme, all things create,
Empires of Earth, of Heaven, of Hell !
To farthest orbs His judgments rang.
As from His lips just sentence fell,
The fetid ranks of Sin shrank down
  Beneath His frown,
Thro' radiant vault of ether sky,

To Hel's domain of misery,
On wings of hideous Nidhögg borne,
In Naströnd's fearful stream to lie,
'Neath serpents' fangs, in lurid flame,
  By Fenrir torn,
Bound fast in adamantine chain
In frightful depths of endless pain ;—
Such was their doom of agony,
  Of fear and shame.

More awful was their second doom.
Exiled forever from His face,
Removēd far in anguished gloom ;
To know, above on starry plain,
In glories shown fair Gimli's fane,
Where joy ecstatic bathed the good
  In endless flood ;
While they, condemned, could gain no place
  E'en at His feet—
Never the faintest ray might snatch,
Nor e'en the dimmest shadow catch
  Of raptures sweet.

Seated, now, in Gimli's portal,
 As before at Asgard's gate,

Fair Iduna, Maid Immortal,
   Shall the purer Æsir wait.
Songs of joyance ever singing,
   Skoals of triumph, sweet and clear,
Thro' the vaulted dome are ringing,
   Echoing thro' crystal sphere.

   " Passed is the gloom of night,
      Finished the fearful fight,
Welcome, thrice welcome ! to glories on high.
      For striving and sadness,
      Now taste ye pure gladness ;
Lo ! thro' the radiant, orient sky,
      From Gimli's wide portal,
      What splendors immortal
Flash o'er your pathway, to Heav'n drawing nigh
      Joy, joy to you, blest ones !
      Behold ! for you gold thrones
Fixed 'neath the dome of Eternity rise ;
      The stars of the morning
      Sing sweet in the dawning !
Rest after conflict, the soul's dearest prize.
      Mount, then, ye heroes all,
      Hasten to Gimli's hall ;
Near you, on golden wing, Victory flies ! "

Pausing awhile, more clear and high
Awoke the notes triumphantly.
On tuneful hinge, with music sweet,
Back roll the gates most glorious
The entering conquerors to greet.
Then, bending from his lofty seat,
  The Judge Supreme,
With smiles that e'er through Gimli gleam,
Now welcomes these, victorious,
Led by Iduna to His feet.

Bowed low before th' Eternal Throne,
A loftier measure still she sings ;
Ten thousand harps with sounding strings
Ascribe all praise to Him alone,
His justice, might and wisdom own.
Thro' list'ning orbs the chorus rings ;
The hosts of Heav'n entrancèd stand
Still in their paths, while echoes grand
Roll in huge waves of ceaseless sound
Those countless burning worlds around.

Too high, too pure, that wondrous strain,
For Earth to catch e'en faint refrain !

Yet still the exultant song rolls on
    For victory won !
The Twilight passed—dread Ragnarock
Passed, with its furious battle shock—
All joyful beams, with brillant ray,
Regeneration's glorious Day !

ALPHABETICAL INDEX OF NOTES.

A.

Ægir.—The Northern Neptune; dwelt on the Isle of Hlesey, where at every harvest he entertained the gods. The last feast given to them was after Baldur's death, ended by the unbidden presence of Loki. Ægir was of giant race, but held intercourse with the gods. He ruled over ocean in its entirety.

Ægir's Daughters.—The waves personified.

Ægir's Sons.—The rain-drops and hail-stones personified.

Æsir.—The gods in Valhalla; of these Odin was chief.

Æsir-Trinity.—Odin, Vili and Vé, sons of Bor, creating the world.

Al-Father.—The supreme God, without a beginning and without end, who should reign in the Regeneration. A title often given to Odin as father of the Æsir.

Angurboda (Anguish-boding).—A giantess, the mother by Loki, of Fenrir, the Serpent, and Hela.

Architect.—The Jotun, who, in disguise, contracted to build a castle of defense to Asgard, in payment to receive Freya, the Sun and Moon. The bargain was made through Loki; nor did the gods see their danger till three days before the castle was completed. Loki, under compulsion, lured away Svadilfari, the chief aid of the Jotun, who in his true form then attacked the gods; he was slain by Thor.

Asgard.—Home of the gods.

Ask.—The Northern Adam; created by the Æsir-Trinity, (Odin, Vili and Vé), from an ash tree.

Audhumla.—The cow formed from the frozen rime of Ginunga. From her udder flowed rivers of milk, on which Ymir was nourished.

B.

BALDUR.—The Summer Sun-God; son of Odin by Friga; best-loved of all gods. Slain by Hodur, through the artifice of Loki.

BERSERKER (WITHOUT ARMOR).—A warrior wild with martial fury; name derived from Arngrim, who, furious, fought unarmed, and conquered the King of Holmgard.

BIFROST.—The Rainbow bridge joining Asgard to Earth; destroyed at Ragnarock by Surtur.

BILSKIRNIR.—The seat of Thor; symbolized the lightning.

BÓR.—Son of Buri, and father of Odin, Vili and Vé, by the Jotun woman, Bestla.

BRAGI.—God of Poetry and Song; son of Odin.

BURI (THE PRODUCER).—The progenitor of the Æsir-Trinity; himself formed by the licking of the salt rime by Audhumla. On the first day, out grew from the stones the hairs of a man; on the second day, the head appeared; and, on the third day, forth sprang the man entire.

D.

DAGR, OR DAY.—Son of Night, by Delling.

DELLING (DAY-BREAK).—Of Æsir race.

DWARFS.—Created out of the dust of the earth by the Æsir-Trinity; of Jotun race, but serving the gods. They dwelt in rocks, chiefly, and were metal-workers. Four of them held up the corners of the sky.

DRAGON'S BED.—A synonym for gold.

DWARFS' DEW.—A synonym for gold.

E.

EAGLE OF IGDRAS L.—Symbol of life, hovering over Igdrasil.

EINHERIAR.—Heroes chosen from battle as allies for Odin agains the Battle of Ragnarock; feasted by him in Valhalla.

ELVIDNIR (THE PLACE OF STORMS).—The hall of Hela in Niflheim.

EMBLA.—The Northern Eve; formed by the Æsir-Trinity from an elm tree.

EYRA.—The goddess of healing; she bound the wounds of the Einheriar in Valhalla.

F.

FENRIR, —Personification of pain, also of earthly fire. Son of Loki by Angurboda. Bred up in Asgard, finally cast out, and bound with Gleipnir, in depths of earth; the foam from his mouth formed the river Von; his tossings caused earthquakes. Through his outstretched jaws the Æsir thrust Odin's sword, the hilt on Earth, the point in Heaven. Loosed in Ragnarock, he swallowed Odin, and was slain by Vidar.

FIMBUL.—The terrible winter which lasted three years, preceding Ragnarock.

FJÖRGYN —Primeval Earth personified. Daughter of Night, and first wife of Odin.

FORSETI.—God of peace and justice. Son of Baldur by Nanna.

FREY.—God of sunshine and soft rains. Of the Vanir, being son of Njörd by Skada; presided over fruitfulness of Earth. His spouse was Gerda, won after long resistance through Skirnir. Their union represented the coming of spring to the winter-Earth. In Ragnarock he was slain by Surtur.

FREYA —The Northern Venus. Goddess of love. Daughter of Njörd by Skada, and next in rank to Friga. The wreath of stars, (Brisingamen) was her necklace; in Folkvang, her hall, she received pure women, and united faithful lovers.

FRIGA.—The Northern Ceres. Daughter of Fjörgyn by Odin, whose wife she became, and queen of the gods. Personification of cultivated Earth. Patroness of industry and conjugal love. She penetrated the future, but could not reveal her knowledge, her lips being sealed by the heron's crown she wore. Foreseeing Baldur's fate, she took from Creation a vow not to injure him, neglecting only the mistletoe. Loki, visiting her as an old woman, discovered this, and hence Baldur's death. Hermoder obtained from Hela a promise to set him free, should all Creation weep for him. Loki as Thökt alone was tearless, and Baldur was lost.

FROST GIANTS, OR HRIMTHURSAR.—-Destructive Jötuns. Deadly influences in nature and in man's soul personified. Sprung from Ymir; they were finally drowned in his blood, save one pair who escaped and became progenitors of new Jötun races

FULLA (FERTILITY).—Maid of Friga, whose casket she bore.

G.

GARM.—Northern Cerberus. Hell-hound guarding Hela's realm. In Ragnarock Tyr and he destroyed each other.

GERDA.—Daughter of the giant Gymer; wife of Frey. Symbol of the aurora-borealis.

GIMLI.—Dwelling of the pure, after Ragnarock.

GINUNGA-GAP.—The abyss of Chaos, placed before creation between Niflheim and Muspelheim; a bottomless chasm, filled with a fermenting mass of formless matter, flowing from the venom streams of Niflheim.

GIÖLL.—One of the venom-rivers, boundary of Hela's realm.

GJALLAR-HORN.—Heimdal's horn.

GLEIPNIR.—The magic chain binding Fenrir; wrought by the dark elves, and brought to the gods by Skirnir.

GNIPA CAVE.—In Niflheim, where was chained Garm.

GOLDEN APPLES.—Given by Iduna to renew youth to the gods.

GONDULA.—One of the Valkyriar.

GRAY WOLF.—Fenrir, Son of Loki.

H.

HEIMDAL.—Northern Iris; warder of Bifröst bridge. Sprung from the nine daughters of the waves, through the glow of Odin's eye. With Gjallar-Horn, he assembled Æsir and Einheriar at Ragnarock, when Loki and he fell together.

HELA.—Daughter of Loki by Angurboda. Goddess of Death, ruling in Niflheim. Divided the dead with Odin, receiving all cowards and evil-doers.

HERMODUR.—Son of Odin by Friga. Messenger of the gods; the Northern Mercury.

HERON'S CROWN (FORGETFULNESS).—Worn by Friga.

HLESEY.—Ægir's abode beneath the ocean.

HŒDUR.—Personification of darkness and ignorance Son of Odin by Friga. Blind slayer of his brother Baldur, by means of the mistletoe dart.

HODMIMIR'S WOOD.—Where the human pair were saved in Ragnarock.

HRÆ.—A giant in eagle guise, stationed in the North, causing storms by the flapping of his wings.

HRIMFAXI.—Steed of Night, scattering frost and dew from his bit.

HRIMTHURSAR.—Frost giants, sprung from Ymir.

HRYM.—The giant steering the ship Nagelfari at Ragnarock.

HRINGHORNI.—The ship upon which Baldur's body was burned. It represented the whole world.

I.

IDAVÖLD, OR IDAVOLLER.—Asgard's plain, where the gods assembled after Creation, and where they met again in the Regeneration.

IDUNA.—Goddess of Immortality; daughter of the dwarf Ivald, and wife of Bragi.

IGDRASIL.—Tree of Life, having three roots, in Niflheim, Jötunheim and Asgard. Mimir's Well was beneath the second, and the Urdar-fount by the last. Nidhögg gnawed the first. Scorched at Ragnarock, it revived in the Regeneration.

J.

JORMUNGANDUR.—The Midgard-Serpent, encircling the Earth; born of Angurboda, by Loki. In Ragnarock, Thor and he fell together.

JOTUNS (GIANTS).—Earliest created beings, sprung from Ymir. Personifications of destructive natural elements and evil passions in man.

JOTUNHEIM (HOME OF GIANTS).—Utgard.

JOTUN-WOLVES.—Pursued Sun and Moon; in Ragnarock, overtook and devoured them.

L.

LAUFEY (LEAF-ISLE).—Mother of Loki.

LJUS-ALFERS.—The light elves; good spirits.

LOKI.—Son of Farbauti by Laufey, and foster-brother of Odin; took part, under the name of Vè, in the creation of man, giving him the senses and passions. In primeval times, he was a benign power. Later, he became the embodied principle of evil. Constant worker of ill to Asgard and Earth. Captured by the gods, and bound with the entrails of his son Narfi, in depths of Earth. Freed in Ragnarock, then slain by Heimdal, who fell also. Earthquakes were thought to be caused by his writhings, and volcanoes by his fiery breath.

M.

MIDGARD.—Earth, formed by the Sons of Bor from the body of Ymir; destroyed in Ragnarock by Surtur's flames, it sprang up more fair in the Regeneration.

MIMIR.—Personification of memory; the all knowing giant keeper of the Well of Wisdom; slain by the Vanir, his head was sent to Odin, who had it embalmed, and thenceforth came to it for advice.

MIMIR's WELL, (THE OCEAN).—Lying beneath the second root of Igdrasil.

MJOLNIR.—Thor's hammer, made for him by the dwarfs.

MODGUD.—The skeleton maid taking toll from the dead who crossed the Gioll. The Northern Charon.

MOON.—Brother of the Sun, and son of the giant Mundilföri, commanded by the gods to drive the car of the Moon. Jotun wolves pursued brother and sister unceasingly, and devoured them at Ragnarock.

MUSPELHEIM.—The realm of flames, ruled over by Surtur. The stars were sparks from Muspelheim.

MUSPEL's SONS.—The flames.

N.

NAGELFARI.—The death-ship built of dead men's nails.

NASTROND.—Place of punishment for the wicked after Ragnarock; in Niflheim.

NIDHOGG.—Symbol of corruption. Death-dragon gnawing the roots of Igdrasil; bore the wicked to Nastrond.

NIFLHEIM.—Existed from the beginning. Ice-cold; the realm of Hela.

NJORD.—A vana-god, patron of sailors and fishermen, and ruling over rains and winds. His wife was Skada; his children were Frey and Freya. He was exchanged by the Vanir for Hœnir, brother of Odin, according to the Elder Edda.

NIGHT.—Daughter of the Jotun Norve. By Delling, of Æsir race, she had a son, Day. Mother and son were placed by Al-father in chariots, and forced to drive successively round the heavens.

NORNIR (SINGULAR, NORNA).—The Fates Goddesses of Time. Represented as three sisters, dwelling at the Urdar-fount, from which they daily watered Igdrasil. Odin himself was forced to seek counsel from them, and obey their decrees.

O.

ODIN.—Son of Bör, by Bestla of Hrymthursar race. The highest of the Æsir-Trinity; from him sprang the other gods in Valhalla. Spirit and essence of the universe. His wives were Jörd, (Fjörgyn) Friga and Rindus, personifications of Earth. In Ragnarock he was destroyed by Fenrir. Wednesday bears his name.

ODIN's EYE (THE SPIRIT)—The Sun. Left in pledge at Mimir's Well, symbolizing the sinking of the sun at night into the ocean; also, the Eye of Heaven, penetrating the depths of Earth. The Spirit seeking out the treasures of memory.

ODIN's RAVENS.—Huginn (mind) and Muninn (memory). Daily bringing him news from all parts of the Earth.

R.

RAGNAROCK.—Destruction of Earth and death of the gods. The final conflict between good and evil powers.

RAN, OR RANA.—Wife of Ægir. Evil and malicious; in her net she caught unwary sailors.

REGENERATION.—Corresponded to the Christian Resurrection. When the High and Mighty One held rule.

RINDUS.—Personification of winter earth. One of Odin's wives.

ROTA.—One of the Valkyriar.

RUNES.—Letters of the old Northern alphabet, supposed to have magical properties.

S.

SAGA.—Goddess of history, dwelling at Sokvabek. Saga, a tale, derives its name from her.

SERPENT.—Jormungandur, son of Loki.

SHIELD-GRAVEN BLOOMS.—The Norsemen decorated the edges of their shields with graven wreaths.

SIF.—Golden-haired wife of Thor, personification of autumn earth covered with harvests.

SIGYN.—Wife of Loki. In his punishment, she held a basin wherein to catch the venom drops otherwise falling on his face.

SKADA.—Wife of Njord, and daughter of Thiassi.

SKALDS.—The bards of the North.

SKINFAXI.—Steed of Day. From his mane, light radiated.

SKIRNIR.—Messenger of Frey.

SKOAL.—Signifies "hail," an expression of greeting.

SKULD.—The Norna of the Future; one of the Valkyriar.

SLEIPNIR.—Foal by Svadilfari of Loki disguised as a mare; with eight legs, and of wonderful swiftness; he became the steed of Odin.

SOKVABEK.—The flowing well, where was the hall of Saga.

SONS OF ÆGIR.—Hail and rain personified.

SURTUR.—The god of fire, guarder of Muspelheim. In Ragnarock, he destroyed Earth with his flames.

SVADILFARI.—Horse of the Jötun architect; sire of Sleipnir.

T.

THIASSI.—Giant father of Skada. For him Loki stole Iduna. He was slain by Thor.

THÖKT (DARKNESS).—Loki, disguised as a giantess, prevented Baldur's ransom.

THOR.—The northern Jupiter; the thunder-god, son of Odin by Fjorgyn, and next in rank to his father. Fell in Ragnarock, poisoned by the Serpent's breath. Represented as young and handsome, with flame-flashing eyes, bent brows (the thunder-cloud), and red beard (lightning). Thursday was named from him.

THUND.—The death-river rolling between Asgard and Earth.

TWILIGHT.—Ragnarock, the fall of the gods.

TYR—God of war; son of Odin, by a giantess; keeper of Fenrir, by him rendered one-handed. Tuesday is named from him.

U.

URDA.—Norna of the Past.

UTGARD.—The capital of Jötunheim.

V.

VALA.—The prophetess; roused from her death-sleep by Odin, she predicted the death of Baldur, and fall of Asgard.

VALHALLA.—Home of the Æsir, where Odin feasted the Einheriar.

VALTAM.—Fictitious name of Odin's father.

VALI.—Son of Odin by Rindus; avenger of his brother Baldur. When only one day old, he slew Hödur. Symbol of the Summer sun chasing away Winter darkness.

VALKYRIAR.—Battle-maidens; choosers of the slain, whom they bore on gory shields to Valhalla, where they served them at Odin's feast.

VANS, OR VANIR.—Gods of the air; deities also of the sea. They were Njörd, Frey and Freya.

VÉ.—Son of Bör. One of the creating Æsir-Trinity.

VEGTAM.—Name assumed by Odin when seeking the Vala.

VERDANDI.—The Norna of the Present.

VIDAR.—Son of Odin by the giantess Grid. In Ragnarock he avenged Odin, and slew Fenrir.

VIGRID.—The field of the final battle in Ragnarock.

VILI.—Son of Bör, and one of the creating Æsir-Trinity.

VINGOLF.—Hall of the goddesses in Asgard.

VIRGIN DAUGHTER OF THE SEA.—Earth, in the Regeneration, uprising from the bosom of the ocean.

Y.

YMIR (THE WORLD MASS)—A giant formed from the melted rime-drops in Ginunga, through the quickening power of the Supreme God. He of himself had the Hrimthursar; was finally slain by the Æsir Trinity, and his sons drowned in his blood. From his parts the world was formed.